A WALKERS' GUIDE TO SUFFOLK

John Pardy

a
CASTELL
publication

RICHARD CASTELL PUBLISHING LIMITED

A WALKERS' GUIDE TO SUFFOLK
COPYRIGHT © 1994 RICHARD CASTELL PUBLISHING LIMITED

ISBN 0 948134 38 0

Text © 1994 John Pardy

First Published June 1994 by
RICHARD CASTELL PUBLISHING LIMITED
Thwaite Eye Suffolk IP23 7EE

Reprinted April 1998

Printed by
THE GIPPING PRESS
Needham Market, Suffolk IP6 8NZ

CONTENTS

Willy Lott's cottage, Flatford. (Walk 8)

INTRODUCTION

THIS BOOK IS A GUIDE for walkers in Suffolk and describes twenty-four walks mainly in the South-East area of the county, each with its own interest and charm. It brings the area and its scenery to life by including more than just the directions for each route. The first part of the book includes a general introduction to the area together with a section on the development of the landscape and how that has affected the modern scene. There are brief geological and historical surveys of the area, of trade and industry in the region and of local flora and fauna.

The bare bones of the route details of each walk are filled out with information of the sort usually found on nature trails. Descriptions of birds and plants likely to be seen during the walk are included. In addition, details are given regarding scenery and local history, and there are brief notes on churches and other historical buildings encountered in each area. Some people are naturally observant and will not need to resort to some of the information given. Seeing and listening in the countryside needs practice, and effort in this respect leads to much greater enjoyment and appreciation of the natural and man-made world around us. I have decided to intertwine notes at the point at which they arise on the ground but these, of course, are by no means exhaustive of all there is to see and discover.

Each walk is circular in route thus avoiding the need for return journeys along the outward path, or wearisome transport arrangements to return to the start point. All the walks were first researched from local O.S. maps to find paths and lanes which provided a circular route without too much use of busy roads. Each was chosen either for its scenery or proximity to market towns or villages likely to be of interest in their own right.

There are preliminary details regarding the start point for a walk with map references, a suitable parking place and approximate distance and time needed for the walk. The time given is generous but does not include time taken out for picnics, birdwatching, wandering around villages, etc..
Names of public houses at convenient half-way or end points are given should a stop for refreshment be needed. Generally I have relied on carrying a snack and can only vouch for the quality of food in a few of the listed 'pubs'!

In the past few years Suffolk County Council and local District and Parish councils have made concerted efforts, with the cooperation of local farmers and landowners, to waymark and publicise footpaths. The result is that many of the walks chosen for this book are clearly signed and waymarked and therefore easy to follow. However, as they cross farm and woodland, the ravages of weather, the development of woods or growing crops can necessitate diversions, and the lush vegetation of summer (including ubiquitous nettles!) can hide signs and block paths. Annual crops can obliterate a footpath temporarily and it may be necessary in the summer to go round a field edge and regain the path on the other side.

A useful companion, therefore, is the relevant O.S. 1 : 50,000 Landranger map for the area to help sort out an alternative path. (It should be remembered that not all the footpaths marked on present maps are Rights of Way today.

Whilst Suffolk is not subject to the extremes of weather encountered in areas such as the Lakes or Dartmoor, certain things should be borne in mind regarding suitable clothing. In wintertime good walking boots are recommended to cope with the ground conditions when crossing farmland, etc. Despite the low rainfall in the area, Suffolk farmland can be very tacky! Some of the walks make use of bridle paths which, with the passage of horses, can be very muddy indeed. As some walks are by the sea or river, remember too that the temperature by water is often lower than that expected inland. The wind-chill factor is also something to be considered before setting out, and it does rain in Suffolk sometimes! In summer twisted ankles on the hard rutted farm tracks or ploughed fields will be avoided by wearing boots or stout shoes.

Details of the Countryside Code are given on page 35. Please do all you can to preserve plant and animal life and to avoid causing problems for all those for whom the countryside is a workplace.

Map Reading. A map reference is given for the beginning of each walk. Remember the first two numbers of the six figures refer to the number at the top or bottom of the map and the fourth and fifth numbers to those at the sides of the map. For the third and sixth numbers imagine that each square of the map is sub-divided into a hundred smaller squares i.e. 10 by 10. If the third and sixth numbers of the reference were 5 that would indicate a point in the middle of the square. Other examples are given on page 122 using a typical map.

The maps needed to cover all the walks in the book are Landranger Nos. 155, 156, 168 and 169. Pathfinder maps Nos. 1053 and 1007 are useful for walks 8 and 10 respectively, but they are not essential.

In my own research for this book I have used a number of useful sources so a bibliography and an index for quick reference is included.

INTO SUFFOLK

THE MAIN TRUNK ROAD of the A12 extends from London diagonally across the bulge of East Anglia to Lowestoft on the coast. It joins Suffolk not far from Dedham where the seventeenth century diarist, Celia Fiennes passed over a wooden bridge to enter the county on her side-saddle journey through Ipswich and on to Blythburgh and Beccles. For many visitors a journey along the A12 road may well provide their first experience of Suffolk, and if so, they could be forgiven for agreeing with the saying 'flat owd Suffolk' and for moving on to more exciting and inspiring scenery. The vast majority of the counties of England, however, have an individuality and richness stemming not just from scenery but also from their historical development, although in Suffolk, as I hope to show later, the latter has been greatly influenced by the nature of the landscape. Of course the impression gained from many main roads can be very misleading - especially now with the construction of by-passes - even amongst such obvious scenic beauty as the Downs or the Lakes.

However a journey along the A12 may reveal two clues to the character of the county which lies on either side. Not long after passing the Essex-Suffolk border the road crosses the River Orwell and, at either end of the modern bridge, motorists may glimpse the view down-river long enough to ponder on its beauty as they speed on. Further along the road edges round the marshland of the River Blyth and one cannot fail to notice the magnificent church at Blythburgh and wonder if it is not some forgotten cathedral. Flat old Suffolk it may be - although the cyclist would sometimes disagree - but the characteristics of river and buildings give a hint of the richness to be found whilst walking in the area.

Further exploration of Suffolk reveals a low, barely undulating country-side with few towns but many interesting villages, a wealth of churches, many houses of architectural interest and an unspoilt coastline intersected by as many as six rivers with their abundant wildlife.

Other characteristics of Suffolk would soon become apparent to travellers who depart from the A12. Journeying down tortuous roads they will pass through parishes of straggling hamlets intersected by open country and pass farms often graced by farmhouses many of which have a medieval origin. Colour washed cottages in pinks and yellows side with those built of brick which may sometimes be of the local Suffolk 'white' variety. The occasional flint cottage and the decorative flint knapping on many churches

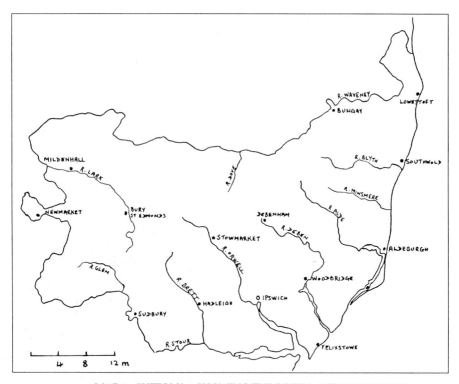

MAP A: SUFFOLK - SHOWING THE RIVERS AND MAIN TOWNS

are a reminder of a rich local building material. Sometimes there seem to be areas of apparent emptiness or a lone church appears on the skyline, a sign of an abandoned village or hamlet. Finally, there is the vast dome of the Suffolk sky. Anyone walking in the area, particularly in the coastal strip of the south-east, cannot fail to sense the 'power' of the 'heavens' in a landscape where obvious features may be few.

Suffolk was the birthplace and inspiration of both Constable and Gainsborough and it was Constable who wrote 'the beauty of the surrounding scenery, its gentle declivities, its luxuriant meadow flats sprinkled with flocks and herds, its well cultivated uplands, its woods and rivers with numerous scattered villages and churches, farms and picturesque cottages, all impart to this particular spot an amenity and elegance hardly anywhere else to be found. 'Perhaps the harsh realities of earning a living in the windswept countryside escaped John Constable, and maybe a truer and more realistic summary is given by Ronald Blythe in his book 'Akenfield'. 'On a clear day - and they are mostly clear in this part of the world - you can see as far as you can bear to see and sometimes farther. It is a suitable climate for a little arable kingdom where flints are its jewels and where existence is sharp-edged'.

The River Stour near Dedham

THE NATURAL LANDSCAPE

THE MODERN LANDSCAPE of Suffolk we see today has evolved naturally over millions of years and man has played a significant part in this only in the last thirty thousand years. To appreciate this modern landscape it is necessary to look back to see how it was first laid down - some acquaintance with local geology provides the key to understanding the countryside and the results of many of man's endeavours in relation to it. The walks chosen for this book are mainly in the area south and east of a line made by the A12. This area which I shall call East Suffolk is markedly different from the rest of the county in several ways and could be described as a natural region on its own. How has this come about?

Geologically, compared with the Highlands or the Dales, Suffolk is the youngster of the British Isles. It is only in the later stages of the geological timetable that the underlying strata of the region was laid down. Reference to the table on the following page shows that a bedrock of chalk was deposited during the Upper Cretaceous period at the end of the Mesozoic era - about one hundred and thirty million years ago. The chalk layer reaches a maximum thickness of 400 metres in Norfolk. Much of southern England and parts of Europe were covered by sea and it was the hard parts of minute floating plants called coccoliths which formed the deposited chalk and which contribute to its fine grain consistency. The lower band of chalk in which ammonites are common, found only near Mildenhall, is more grey or pink in colour and flintless. Above that the middle band varies in consistency and carries a few flints, and again this band only rises to the surface in the west of the county. The upper chalk which contains many more flints is white and much softer, and this band is evident in parts of the Gipping Valley. (Walk 10) The flints which are concentrations of pure silica - formed from sponges and other tiny marine creatures - occur in layers or bands of nodules which formed after the chalk was laid down. They were to become a major building and decorative material of many churches and buildings in East Anglia. The chalk is at its thickest in Norfolk, and in Suffolk it is raised in the West to slope gently towards the coast. The coast at that time lay in a line extending roughly from Sudbury north-east to Stowmarket, and through Eye to Lowestoft. Earth movements resulted in the gently rolling countryside of this area as we see it today.

Later, about sixty million years ago, Norfolk and Suffolk were submerged beneath the sea and during the Cenezoic era the clays that make up the London Clays and the Reading Beds were laid down together with the

THE GEOLOGICAL TIME CHART

Millions of years ago	Begins Period	Era	Events
1.8	Quaternary		Anglian ice sheet. Period of glaciations
5	Pliocene		
22.5	Miocene	Cenezoic	
38	Oligocene Tertiary		Alps and Himalayas formed.
54	Eocene		
65	Palaeocene		
			Chalk deposits formed. Evolution of flowering plants.
141	Cretaceous		
195	Jurassic	Mesozoic	
230	Triassic		Dinosaurs dominant
280	Permian		Coal seams laid down.
345	Carboniferous		
395	Devonian	Palaeozoic	
435	Silurian		
500	Ordovician		Volcanic activity in Wales & Lakes.
570	Cambrian		
2500	Pre-Cambrian		Pre-history of Scotland.

Coralline Crag which is exposed near Orford. London Clay lies beneath the crag of the Orwell and Deben esturies and the clays of the Reading Beds underlie the valley of the River Gipping. (See map B, next page).

The end of the Pliocene period saw the accumulation of shelly sands and crags containing fossils which indicate the sudden cooling and beginning of the Ice Age.

The Quaternary period which followed was one of glacial advances and recessions, a sequence of cooling and warmer periods. Glaciers which formed in the North moved south bringing with them clay and chalk and collecting the clays and crags laid down previously in Norfolk and Suffolk. (Many sources refer to four glaciations occurring during this period although modern research disputes that there is any real evidence for this.)

The warmer climate of the south meant that the glaciers were melting as they moved and the rush of water brought with it mud, sands and gravels. These were deposited along the coastal area of Suffolk extending from Southwold in the north to Felixstowe in the south and in the valley of the River Gipping covering the boulder clays beneath.

It is thought that the final ice sheet retreated from the area about 10,000 years ago - in geological terms a very brief span of time. Suffolk had gained its present shape except for the land bridge extending to the continent. A very low sea level meant that the land mass extended and joined to the Low Countries and the North Sea coastline was 150 miles further north. Suffolk's rivers were tributaries of the Thames which itself joined the Rhine to flow into the North Sea, north of the area of the present Dogger Bank. About 6000 B.C. with the warmer climate, the melting glaciers and rising sea level drowned the land bridge to the continent and Britain became an island. Gradually the coastline advanced and Suffolk's shape formed into the one we recognise today. Apart from the estuary of

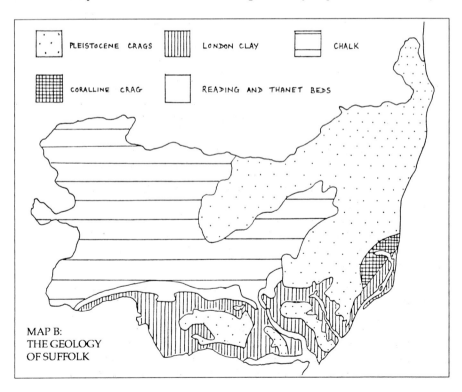

MAP B:
THE GEOLOGY
OF SUFFOLK

PLEISTOCENE CRAGS   LONDON CLAY   CHALK

CORALLINE CRAG   READING AND THANET BEDS

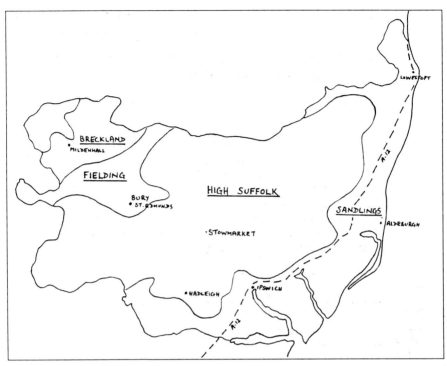

MAP C: THE FOUR MAIN AREAS OF SUFFOLK

the River Ore which was formed by tidal drift, the estuaries of the other Suffolk rivers were formed during the flooding of the river valleys.

Rich chalky boulder clays or 'glacial till' were left by the retreating glaciers in West and Mid-Suffolk. The scouring action of the glaciers not only formed the river valleys and the localised Suffolk 'gulls' but also caused other local variations such as the exposure of the underlying chalk in the Gipping valley and the red crag in East Suffolk. Crag is a local term for the shelly sand-like loam of the area.

The deposits formed the landscape we see today. As a result Suffolk can be divided into four main regions as shown on Map C. The man-made A12 trunk road neatly divides the county into the two main geological areas, the boulder clays of Mid and West Suffolk called High Suffolk - in 1735 John Kirby named the area as The Woodlands - and the coastal belt of sandy gravels or Sandlings of East Suffolk. North-West Suffolk, or the Brecklands, was the third part. (Kirby's 'The Fieldings'.) The Sandlings are

13

intersected by the river valleys of the Orwell, Deben, Alde and Blyth, together with the Stour which forms a natural boundary in the south. It is this area of East Suffolk which the motorist on the A12 will notice, and only if he turns north-west will the rolling nature of the remainder of Suffolk become more apparent.

The natural landscape has, of course, evolved not least because of the attentions of man, but as will be seen shortly, man's influence on the Suffolk scene has largely been determined by the basic difference between the boulder clays of Mid-Suffolk which proved rich for farming and the more arid sands of the coastal area. These were, until reclamation by the use of crag in Victorian times, and chemical fertilisers more recently, heaths, useful only for grazing sheep and the breeding of rabbits.

The basic principle of geology is that the earth is constantly changing and it is fascinating to attempt to project what shape Suffolk will be in the distant future. Will there be another Ice Age to transform the landscape? Certainly during the last five hundred years there has been much coastal erosion as evident at Dunwich (Walk 3), but there has been much growth too. W.G.Arnott estimates the annual loss of coastline to be about 46cms and the Orford spit to have grown five and a half miles in seven hundred years. Half of this has occurred in the last three hundred years. By a process called longshore drift, eroded shingle has been moved southwards and so Orfordness continues to lengthen. Other shingle banks are already changing the shape of the estuary of the River Deben. In addition Man has played a part in eroding and adding to the landscape and this is the subject of the next chapter.

MAN AND THE LANDSCAPE

THE INFLUENCE OF MAN in Britain extends only about 300,000 years. Discovery of hand-axes and the examination of pollen remains at Hoxne near the Suffolk-Norfolk border show that early man existed here for a while. Extensive colonisation, however, did not occur until the end of the glacial period. The warmer climate that followed the last Ice Age had had its effect on the landscape and by the time of man's arrival the whole region was covered by natural wildwood. Survival depended upon woodland clearance and that was what very early man did, probably by burning. Before the Neolithic period Suffolk was 'woodland with holes'. Later, clearance became easier with the mining and production of flint tools, many from Grimes Graves, an extensive area of flint mines near Thetford totalling three hundred and sixty-six pits in all. Before then man survived mainly by hunting the many wild animals that roamed the wildwood, but a more settled existance with the farming of crops now became possible.

Modern archaeological research tends to the view that the English landscape that we see today is much older than was thought even by W.G.Hoskins in his pioneering book on the subject. For example, the clearance of the original woodland that covered Suffolk is thought to have taken place much earlier than he estimated. Clearance began about 8000 B.C. and by the time of the Norman invasion in 1066 there was little natural woodland left other than what was managed or what had naturally regenerated. Rackham estimates that half of England ceased to be covered in wildwood by 500 B.C. which could be rated an achievement considering the tools available then and the fact that most British species of tree are difficult to kill! The demand for land for cultivation and, to a lesser extent, the need for wood for the building of huts and more sophisticated dwellings would certainly have led to the decimation of much woodland. The development of the flint industry in Neolithic times of which Grimes Graves was just one example - axes from Cornish mines have been found in south-east Suffolk - helped the process of felling which grew apace later with the introduction of bronze and iron.

Another factor was a sudden expansion of the population in the late Bronze Age, 1800 B.C., which led to the growth of more settlements and the consequent need to reclaim and develop more land. The population of England is estimated to have risen from a few thousand in 5000 B.C. to 50,000 in 2500 B.C., and by 1200 B.C. there were approaching one million. This could have doubled by the time of the Roman occupation. (Research has shown that East Anglia was particularly affected by this explosion, evident from the large number of burial mounds dating from the period. (There is a concentration of these in South-East Suffolk, particularly in the areas bordering the Stour, Orwell and Deben rivers.)

The result, therefore, was that by the time of the Roman invasion the general pattern of our landscape was laid down. Not only had a large proportion of the wildwood been cleared but the majority of settlements, tracks and boundaries, land systems and the framework of fields were in existence. The Romans added to and developed what was already there. Market towns developed near existing settlements, and roads from ancient trackways. In the area covered by this book, large settlements or market towns grew up at Capel, Felixstowe, Coddenham, Hacheston, Knodishall and Wenhaston, and these were surrounded by many farmsteads some of which were graced by large villas. Suffolk, being on the through route from the large military town of Colchester to the Norfolk town of Caister, benefited from the increased trade that resulted. So, "when the Saxons finally arrived in England they came not to an empty land of forests, marshes and moorland, but to a crowded, totally exploited country covered in fields, roads, towns, villages and farmsteads all organised into a complex system of landholding and with political, administrative and religious boundaries not only fixed but of great antiquity." (C.Taylor)

The extent of woodland clearance in earlier times was affected by the essential geological difference of the two main areas of Suffolk. Clearance and cultivation of the light soils in the east was initially easier but this led to erosion of the surface soils to leave the sands and gravels of the area now known as the Sandlings. Later, farming of sheep and rabbits was the only economical proposition. The open heaths and sheepwalks of the Sandlings have now nearly all disappeared (It is interesting that the present century saw the reafforestation of large areas of the Sandlings, parts of which were decimated in the hurricane of 1987. See Walk 6.)

On the heavier clays of mid-Suffolk it proved more difficult and slower to clear and cultivate. At first settlements grew up in small clearings or within easy reach of water for cattle but with the arrival of the Belgae tribes in the first century B.C., and the heavy plough, wider clearance became possible. A thousand years later, Domesday Book records that the mid-Suffolk claylands had the greatest density of plough teams - four to the square mile. Then, as now, this area provided the richer farmland. Also the general area was called 'the Woodlands' as late as 1735, so presumably there was still enough woodland left, albeit patchy, to warrant the name.

By the seventh century the population of England had declined from a possible four million at the end of the Roman era to between two and three million. It is thought that the 'invasion' of the Saxons, coming from what is now northern Germany, did not increase the population by more than 100,000 and maybe much less. Suffolk, providing the nearest landfall, may well have had the larger influx. Like earlier settlers they tended to concentrate on the coast and by the side of the river valleys along which they had arrived. Archaeologists have not as yet detailed information about the origin of many villages but it seems obvious to conclude that the invaders, as well as establishing many new settlements, also made use of and developed existing ones. Excavations have shown that it is possible to date the origin of Ipswich from this time.

What seems certain is that by the time of the Domesday record the general pattern and outline of the county was established and until the present century the area did not undergo great changes. Nearly all the 500 parish names recorded in Domesday show that Suffolk must have been one of the richer areas of the country and it remained so until the end of the sixteenth century. It was one of the most thickly populated and with 7,460 freemen recorded in Domesday - more than half the total for the rest of the country - the economy of the county was strong.

Further evidence for this may be deduced from the wealth of churches in existance. Norman Scarfe has counted 417 Suffolk churches recorded in Domesday Book. He writes, "Nowhere else in Britain is it at all feasable to go out into the country, look around at so impressive an array of churches, and know that you are looking at points fixed on the human landscape even before that decisive battle on 14 October 1066." (The Suffolk Landscape) It is said that on a clear day fifty church towers can be seen from the tower of Wickham Market Church although the author has not tested this!

141 more churches were built in the Middle Ages and most of the existing pre-Norman churches were to be rebuilt and enlarged in that period, a sign of continuing wealth. Nearly five hundred medieval churches remain in Suffolk today out of fifteen thousand in England. Not only are they some of the best in the country but also they are one of the many outstanding features of the county that give it its appeal.

In the early sixteenth century Suffolk was the fourth wealthiest county in England after Kent, Devon and Norfolk, and Ipswich was the sixth richest town. Suffolk's wealth at this time arose from the manufacture of woollen cloth, and merchants and others who benefited were only to keen to endow their local churches or to finance their extension and development adding to their splendour. Benefactors such as the Howards and the DeVeres saw to the enlargement and refurbishing of churches in the Perpendicular style

There was enthusiasm for going one better than the neighbouring church and smaller parishes copied designs from others as at Walberswick. (Walk 17) There, records show that the tower was not built in a year, partly no doubt on account of inclement winter weather, but also because of the quality of the mortar used. Time was needed for the mortar to harden and so building was done in stages. Ten feet in height a year was a rough norm, so the Walberswick tower may well have taken ten years to complete. The mason building the tower at Helmingham Church was allowed ten years to build sixty feet.

Not every parish was fortunate to receive enough donations and bequests to complete building work. There is evidence that churches held 'Ales' to raise extra funds - the equivalent of the modern bring and buy, bazaars, or the cycle rides pioneered by the Suffolk Historic Churches Trust.

Isolated churches abound in Suffolk. A thriving population could not always survive on the poor soil of the Sandlings. On the clay soils of mid-Suffolk, isolated churches were often part of very small parishes and arose because the centre of the village shifted away from the church for various reasons. At Martlesham, for instance, the church tops a hill overlooking the nearby creek and the River Deben - a good vantage point for an early settlement. But the centre of the village is now a mile or more away astride what was the A12. It probably developed there about 1785 when the highway became a busy turnpike road from Ipswich to Lowestoft. (There was a toll bar in the vicinity of the Red Lion inn.) Not every church, though, had its origins in the centre of the village. Some were associated with a local estate or manor which lay outside the area around which the village grew.

Not only were the sites of churches established by 1066, Domesday recorded nine market towns, five of which were in the south-eastern area: Ipswich, Dunwich, Blythburgh, Kelsale and Stowmarket. By 1547 ninety-eight towns and villages had grants to hold a market. No doubt many of these were expedients to raise money for the central exchequer and some may not have survived for long. It seems strange now to know, for instance, that Shotley and Erwarton (Walk 7) were granted rights to hold markets in 1303 and 1347 respectively when only a mile or two separate them on the map. Were they on different days of the week or did their proximity to busy river traffic justify their existence?

By the seventeenth century there were 36 mediaeval markets still existing in Suffolk and twelve of these were in the south-eastern area: Nayland, Hadleigh, Ipswich, Woodbridge, Wickham Market, Orford, Aldeburgh, Saxmundham, Framlingham, Blythburgh, Dunwich and Southwold.

Fairs were very much an aspect of mediaeval Suffolk, there being over ninety and many outlasted the markets. By the end of the eighteenth century there were over one hundred, although only two in the Sandlings, at Orford and Aldeburgh. Some of these were very specialised; Hacheston known for its footwear, upholstery and joinery. Prior to the Great War, however, the number of fairs had dwindled to thirteen.

The names of many Suffolk villages recorded in Domesday are those which exist today; Car's Eye (Kersey), Merlesham (Martlesham), Buclesham (Bucklesham), Tremelaia (Trimley), Wdebregge (Woodbridge), to name but a few. The earliest place names are thought to be those with a topographical origin i.e. Car's Eye meaning a stream running into a brook; Tremelaia (Tryma's Leah) an island or woodland clearing.

By 1200 the layout of many villages had taken shape. Suffolk seems to have a mixture of street linear villages (those which stretch out along a single road) and green villages centred around a village green. The latter are mainly to be found in High Suffolk and were deliberately planned probably by the local lord - the green being the area used for common pasture. Mellis near Eye is a good example. Street villages arose from gradual accretions to an existing settlement - a kind of squatting. Hacheston village, near Framlingham (Walk 12), for example, stretches for a mile. The common or pasture land, available to all, lay alongside.

A feature of Suffolk which will be noted by the walker is the large number of moated farmhouses and halls. These are very largely to be found on the heavy claylands of the Woodlands or mid-Suffolk, stretching as they do diagonally in a broad band from the south-west to the north-east. It was thought that a moat was a means of keeping the top-soil dry for the dwelling it surrounded - an essential feature in areas which quickly became waterlogged in the winter. However, Oliver Rackham, in his book, disputes this as a reason for building a moat and argues that they were a status symbol and built for ornamental reasons. The majority of the sites were built in the thirteenth century although the Elizabethan era saw a revival of the fashion. A good example is the beautiful moated Hall at Parham built in the fifteenth and sixteenth centuries on the site of a previous fortified manor house. (Walk 12) The majority of moats enclose less than an acre of land and usually the barns and outbuildings lay outside the moat. Some houses, like Parham, have impressive gatehouses.

Another characteristic of the area linked to the poor drainage of the claylands is the large number of ponds to be found alongside farmhouses, acting as a land drain and also providing a watering place for cattle and a home for duck, etc. Now, of course, these ponds are an important part of the natural environment.

What of the woodland that survived the clearance by early man? Oliver

Rackham estimates that, at the time of Doomsday, only 9% of Suffolk was still woodland and what survived the mediaeval period is mainly to be found in the south-west. Groton Wood, near Hadleigh, is a possible survival. (A study of lichens in a wood can reveal its age) What remained in Medieval times were in defined areas and were carefully managed on behalf of the local abbey, lord or squire who owned the land. Properly coppiced, as many were, they provided a regular supply of wood for tools and fences and, from the standard trees, timber for building. Whilst areas were set aside for common grazing of swine or pannage, others provided good hunting cover. The Priory at Butley (Walk 9) owned the nearby Staverton Park, which is an example of a surviving deer park developed after the Norman Conquest. This was one of the few examples of an original medieval park that survive to this day and is now known as Staverton Thicks. The name Staverton (Stavertuna in Domesday) comes from the old English meaning a farm enclosed by stakes. Today this ancient park contains several thousand pollard oaks and some ancient holly trees. (The park is private and although it is not possible to walk through it, a footpath does skirt the edge.) There are many other parks in Suffolk but a great number are later ornamental parks of the seventeenth and eighteenth centuries, the one at Helmingham being a good example.

Mention has been made of the results of woodland clearance on the Sandling area of Suffolk and the consequent rise of sheep farming which lasted until this century. There are many references to sheep 'walks' on O.S.Maps. Examination of maps will also reveal many 'warrens', evidence of a thriving industry in farming rabbits. Heaths were maintained to preserve the local warrens and in the leases for manors a condition was to leave warrens well stocked. Robert Ryece, in his description of Suffolk written in 1603, spoke of the rich profits to be made from rabbits by all good housekeepers. "There is none who deem their houses well seated who have not to the same belonging a common wealth of coneys". In the lease for the manor of Westwood near Blythburgh in 1499, the warren was to be left 'well replanished with two thousand conyes or more'. In 1701, one thousand five hundred rabbits a year were sent to the landlord. Needless to say, Warren and Warrener are common names in Suffolk!

The decline in the rabbit population began early this century with the change in farming methods and land reclamation for forestry, and the consequent loss of heathland was accelerated more recently with the building of airfields and housing. In the first sixty or so years of this century, the nineteen thousand acres of heathland between Ipswich and Lowestoft were reduced to eight thousand four hundred. Myxomatosis was an added factor leading to changes in the ecology of the remaining heaths by allowing the growth of more grass, birch and scrub. The loss of heathland habitat has also led to a decline in several species of bird such as nightjar, stone curlew and Dartford warbler.

The Parliamentary enclosure of land which took place in the rest of the country in the eighteenth and nineteenth centuries did not have such a marked effect in East Suffolk as elsewhere. Enclosure of land had taken place much earlier in Tudor times, and even then it is doubtful whether much was left to enclose. The boulder clay lands of mid-Suffolk were largely enclosed by the end of Elizabeth's reign. Many fields were 'enclosed' early in the Middle Ages and surrounded by deep ditches and banks for drainage which have, over the years, come to look part of the natural landscape.

What was left to enclose in Georgian times were tracts of common land mostly in the east. The land bordering the road between Woodbridge and Felixstowe, near Bucklesham, is one example, and the large area of Sutton Common (Walk 13) is another. Quick growing hawthorn was much favoured for the hedges that were planted and this was partnered by blackthorn which grows well on clay soil, or by privet and elder which thrive on chalky and sandy soils.

What of more recent times? The large-scale removal of hedges in East Anglia in the 1960's to allow for more efficient farming methods did not bear so heavily in Suffolk as it did in Norfolk, except in the north of the county, but nevertheless the ecological damage was extensive (see the section on the natural environment).

However, history shows that farming methods have changed as the health of the economy has altered. For example, owing to changing corn prices, two and a half million acres of arable land were laid to grass in the late nineteenth century. Over a hundred years later land is being set aside because of over-production of cereals and no doubt this will have a noticeable effect on the landscape.

The arrival of the railways and the development of the motor car industry have obviously had their effect on the area but generally Suffolk remains very much a rural county. The railways came to Suffolk in the 1850's and the line from Ipswich to Felixstowe as late as 1877. This led to considerable expansion of towns like Ipswich, Bury St. Edmunds and Lowestoft, and indeed was responsible for the growth of Felixstowe from a small village to a thriving seaside town. Similarly with roads. The network of rural lanes and tracks were to be the basis for the modern roads, and the turnpikes of the eighteenth century became the A12 and A45 trunk roads. These two largely bear the brunt of Suffolk's traffic leaving the remainder of the county relatively uncrowded.

HISTORICAL EVENTS IN SUFFOLK

THE FOLLOWING SECTION is a brief account of the historical development of Suffolk with particular reference to the area covered by the walks in this book.

- 6500 B.C. Before this time East Anglia was linked to the continent and the area experienced intermittent waves of hunters from 'abroad'. Short periods of settlement gradually became longer as the area finally emerged from a series of glaciations. The only site which is thought to pre-date the Anglian ice sheet is at Mildenhall in the north-west of the county. The ice sheet covered all of Suffolk except the south-east which is subject to Siberian type weather conditions. Hunting parties may have visited between glaciations or maybe they adapted to the extreme conditions. Flint heads recovered from near Hoxne point to a settlement which existed thirty thousand years ago, and discoveries of flints in the gravels of the River Gipping valley point to the presence of hunters. The landscape was dominated by wildwood.

c.6500 B.C. England becomes an island and Suffolk begins to assume its present shape. Barbed hunting weapons of the late Mesolithic period are discovered at Barham.

4600 B.C. There is evidence of the first settled communities raising cattle and arable crops at Freston near Ipswich and at Stratford St Mary where remains of pottery and axes were discovered.

2000 B.C. Settled farming communities are now much in evidence. The industry of flint mining in the area of Grimes Graves is at its height with the demand for tools suitable for forest clearance as well as for hunting. (Research has shown that it was possible to cut down a pine tree of 15cm diameter with a flint axe in five minutes.) There are settlements in the Ipswich area. Ancient trackways become well established.

1700 B.C. There are many round burial mounds on Foxhall and Martlesham heaths which point to large Bronze age settlements near Ipswich at this time. Over seven hundred existed in Suffolk, but only about one hundred are visible today, many only from the air. The mounds are concentrated in the Sandlings. Many more mounds probably existed only to be destroyed by ploughing later. Their absence in High Suffolk is explained by the difficulty of forest clearance on the heavier soil.

1000 B.C. There are now settled farming communities. The Trinovantes tribe inhabit the South Suffolk area and the Stour valley with the Iceni in the north. Cultivation of the land becomes easier with the arrival of the iron plough. Most sites are near water and there are very few in the Sandlings which possibly proved too dry.

50 B.C.   The Roman era.

Over four hundred miles of roads are built in Suffolk although the Romans use the routes of old trackways. From their headquarters in the main town of Camulodunum (Colchester) a Roman road enters Suffolk at Stratford St Mary and continues to Coddenham (Combretonium) where a camp is established on the route to Venta Icenorum (Caister St Edmund, near present-day Norwich). A branch road from Coddenham may have led to Dunwich. There are large settlements at Capel, Hacheston, Knodishall, Wenhaston and Felixstowe, some of these possibly acting as supply distribution centres. A pottery is established at Wattisfield. The Iceni live peaceably under Prasutagus but rebel under his widow Boudicca. The rebellion is ruthlessly crushed and the town of Colchester sacked.

300 A.D.   Forts are established at Burgh Castle, near Great Yarmouth, and at Walton, Felixstowe to counter the early Saxon invasions.

400 - 1000 A.D.   The Engles (Anglo-Saxons) establish a new homeland - perhaps the true beginning of the English nation and its political institutions. German mercenaries from the Roman army may well have remained to live after the Romans withdrew. Colonisation by invaders at first concentrated near rivers (e.g. near Felixstowe and Butley).

The hundreds of Babergh, Colneis, Claydon, Wilford, Blything, Wangford, Bosmere, Hartismere and Samford were established during this period. (see Map D) The framework of towns and villages which we know today originates from this period. Ipswich is founded, and there are markets there and at Dunwich. Felix becomes Bishop of Dunwich and monasteries are founded there, at Burgh and Bury - and possibly at Iken by St Botolph. The Wuffingas, the ruling family in the area to which Raedwald belonged (see Sutton Hoo walk) are baptised into Christianity in 620, possibly retaining some of their pagan beliefs at the same time.

During the nineth century the Danes make incursions into the area, attacking Ipswich in 991 and again in 1010. A ditch is dug to defend the town thus giving an area of the modern town the name of Tower Ramparts. The village of Eyke, near Woodbridge, derives from the Danish, meaning a settlement near woods.

1000 - 1200 A.D.   The Norman Period.

The dissent shown by Boudicca earlier in East Anglia is repeated, this time by Hereward the Wake in the Fens. Suffolk is parcelled out between fewer than twenty barons.

Domesday records the population as twenty thousand. Mound castles are built at Otley and Haughley and more lasting castles were built later, notably at Orford and at Framlingham to quell unrest. There are markets at Blythburgh and Stowmarket. Ecclesiastical administration is organised in deaneries with similar boundaries to the 'hundreds', some with the same name e.g. Samford, Colneis, Carlford and Wilford. More religious communities are founded - Butley Priory is established in 1171. More monasteries exist in this area because large tracts of land and manors are owned by the Abbey at Bury. The wool trade begins with Flanders. The Earl of Leicester's army of ten thousand Flemings is defeated near Bury in 1173. A Royal charter is given to Ipswich in Richard I's reign. At Framlingham in 1214, earls and barons take an oath withdrawing loyalty to King John.

MAP D: THE SUFFOLK HUNDREDS

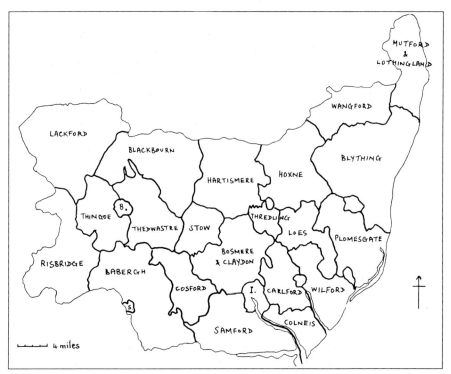

1300 - 1500 The Black Death proves to be severe in East Anglia. Fify-seven thousand are estimated to have died in Suffolk and Norfolk. Many parishes have to appoint a new priest. The resulting labour shortage and poor wages leads to local uprisings during the Peasant's Revolt in 1381. Property was destroyed at Ipswich and East Bergholt, and at Hollesley, in June there is a public burning of manorial documents from Butley Abbey as a strike for freedom from villeinage. Monastic power and wealth causes other disputes. The monastery at Bury is attacked by a crowd of twenty thousand from the town and the surrounding villages. Cartloads of rioters are sent to Norwich and nineteen are executed. Towns expand and the number of markets increases; charters are awarded, especially to places near the coast and bordering rivers. European links are strengthened by the wool trade and Flemish artisans come to this country to teach the skills of spinning, weaving, etc.. The Feudal system collapses earlier in the area with the growth of money wages and development of trade gilds.

Local ports like Harwich, Orford and Dunwich compare favourably with larger ports such as Bristol by supplying ships to support Edward III's war with France.

1500 - 1600 Poverty in Suffolk is marked by a rebellion in 1525 in Hadleigh and other Suffolk towns when crowds protest at a new tax by Cardinal Wolsey. The Dukes of Suffolk and Norfolk meet protesters at Bury. Hadleigh is the third richest town in Suffolk after Ipswich and Bury. Lax administration and corruption in local monasteries leads to their dissolution under Wolsey. St. Peter's Priory and small monasteries at Felixstowe and Snape are closed. Many churches sell valuables to avoid seizure by the King. A Grammar school is endowed at Ipswich.

During the reign of Queen Mary, persecution of heresy in East Anglia is intense. In 1515 Dr. Rowland Taylor is executed at Hadleigh, two are burnt at Debenham, and others on Cornhill in Ipswich. More dissenters are imprisoned in Framlingham Castle. Queen Elizabeth tours Suffolk 1578-9. She allows measures to protect Protestant exiles. Woodbridge benefits from the endowments of a wealthy merchant, Thomas Seckford, who provides a school and almshouses.

1600 - 1700 The history of dissent that started with Boudicca in Roman times continues in East Anglia.

1630 Many East Anglians join the emigrants to New England. John Winthrop, from Groton near Sudbury, becomes Governor of Massachusetts. Ipswich is a centre for Puritanism and strict rules are enforced for Sunday behaviour.

1636 The Society of Friends is founded by John Fox in Norwich while, in the same year, Sir Robert Hitcham leaves money for the education of the poor in Debenham.

The tranquil Gipping nr. Baylham. Once a thriving canel linking the rural heartland with Ipswich port.

Was the Civil War born in the region? Dissent in religious matters fuels the political and economic unrest. Ship money is a particular burden on local ports struggling to compete with ports elsewhere.

The Eastern Counties Association is made up of merchant gentlemen with strong Protestant traditions. Parliamentarians are in the majority in East Suffolk and in High or mid-Suffolk. Puritan influence is strong in Ipswich. During the war there is little action in Suffolk apart from a local riot at Stoke by Nayland. Ipswich receives advice from Colchester regarding defensive precautions after the siege there in 1648. Fear of witches in Suffolk results in the burning of Mother Lakeland in Ipswich in 1645. She was said to have sold herself to the devil. The endeavours of the witchfinder, Matthew Hopkins, resulted in the hanging of forty in Bury and sixty throughout Suffolk including an old clergyman and his wife. John Lowes, the Vicar of Brandeston, is accused of witchcraft and hung at Bury. Aldeburgh incurs a bill for £6.7s for Hopkins' board and witchfinding services.

William Dowsing's activities during the Protectorate cover a wide area in Suffolk. "At Stoke we broke down a hundred superstitious pictures". Ipswich churches took two days to clear of offending decoration so they

were, no doubt, glad to welcome the return of Charles 11. His coat of arms
hangs in St. Margaret's Church in the town. There is growing freedom of
thought in the county.
Navy press gangs were at work in Woodbridge, Orford and Aldeburgh
during 1652.

1700 - 1900 Defoe travels by coach to London in ten hours in 1762. By 1829
there are 278 miles of turnpike roads in Suffolk. Canals improve commu-
nications. The population of Stowmarket had doubled by 1855 following
the opening of the Gipping canal in 1793.

Few Parliamentary Enclosure Acts apply to Suffolk; much of High Suffolk
is arable land mainly given over to dairy farming and had been enclosed
in medieval times. High corn prices during the Napoleonic Wars encourage farmers to plough up land for wheat and barley crops. Sheep farming
is concentrated in East Suffolk with four-hundred thousand sheep compared with a tenth of that number of cattle.
Railways come late to Suffolk. The route to Ipswich is completed in 1846.
The first train to Colchester stops at Bentley to be welcomed by represen-
tatives of local villages. The line to Bury which involved the construction
of a hundred bridges is built in just over one year. The opening of the line
to Lowestoft in 1859 and to Felixstowe in 1877 leads to the rapid growth of
each town's prosperity. The narrow gauge line from Halesworth to
Southwold opens in 1879.

1900 - 1993 The arrival of the railways and later the motor car results in
the decline of canals and local railway lines. Stowmarket canal was
disused by 1922 and Southwold railway line closes in 1929. In 1973 the
county is united administratively by the formation of the new Suffolk
County Council which assumed the responsibilities of the old East and
West Suffolk and Ipswich Borough Councils. The County is divided into
six district Councils of which Babergh, Mid-Suffolk and Suffolk Coastal
cover the area walked and described in this book.

TRADE AND INDUSTRY

ONE OF THE OLDEST INDUSTRIES must be that associated with flint mining carried on at Grimes Graves near Thetford, on the Norfolk-Suffolk border, to equip neolithic man with necessary tools and weapons. Much later, flints were used for building and there was a demand for knapped flints for decorating churches and large houses in the Middle Ages through to Victorian times. There was also an upsurge in flints in the late eighteenth century during the Napoleonic Wars. Knapped flints were even used on the exterior of British Telecom's research building at Martlesham when it was built in the early 1970's.

Throughout the Bronze Age there was considerable trade with the Low Countries in bronze, pottery and wine. During the Roman occupation there was a pottery at Wattisfield. Salt was produced in river estuaries, for instance, at Trimley and at Iken, and there was a trade in wool. In Saxon times, Ipswich became a centre for pottery and, following the conversion of East Anglia to Christianity, the skills associated with the production of cloth and embroidery flourished.

Domesday Book records the existence of one hundred and seventy eight water mills in Suffolk which illustrates the extent of arable farming in the area.

Flour milling, malting and brewing, and fishing were expanding industries in the Middle Ages, and both Woodbridge and Dunwich became famous for boat building. Pilgrimage sites brought an influx of people to Bury. A cottage industry grew up for wool, but the immigration of craftsmen from the Low Countries led later to the development of a cloth industry. The River Stour provided excellent sites for fulling mills and Hadleigh and the surrounding towns in West Suffolk became wealthy as cloth making towns. Ipswich became the centre for exporting their goods. This industry led, as noted elsewhere, to the building and endowment of many of Suffolk's fine churches. Later, when the broad cloth industry declined owing to the production of lighter fabrics in the mills of Yorkshire and Lancashire, a silk industry developed as well as straw plaiting for the making of hats.

Agriculture was centred mainly on dairy farming in High Suffolk. Daniel Defoe wrote that the area "was famous for the best butter and perhaps the worst cheese in England". Much of the produce in the seventeenth and eighteenth centuries was sent to London, but he wrote, "the butter is baralled or often pickled up in small casks and sold, not only in London but I have known a firkin of Suffolk butter sent to the West Indies and brought back to England again, and has been perfectly good and sweet as at first".

He described Orford as "once a good town but now decayed . . . it should be a seaport no longer". He noted this was due to the action of the sea in blocking off the river. Of Ipswich he wrote, "I take this town to be one of the most agreeable places in England", and he proceeded to give six reasons, amongst which was a plentiful supply of good provisions and "an easy passage to London either by land or water". He also mentioned the large droves of turkeys and geese that were driven across the bridge over the Stour at Stratford St. Mary on their way to be sold in London.

William Cobbett in his tour of 1830 mentions the immense quantities of corn grown in the county, the innumerable windmills in the area that converted the corn into flour and the neat and well-kept farmhouses. "I have always found Suffolk farmers great boasters of their superiority over others and I must say that it is not without reason."

The predominance of cattle in High Suffolk led to a strong leather industry. The agricultural produce not only boosted Ipswich and the other ports of Suffolk but provided the basis for a flourishing engineering industry. Robert Ransome, the forerunner of the present Ransome Sims and Jefferies, started his Ipswich business in 1789 patenting cast-iron ploughshares, and later, the first lawnmower. Boosted by the discovery of coprolites, the firm of Fisons was founded in 1847. At Leiston in the nineteenth century, Richard Garrett began producing agricultural machinery of all kinds and later on developed the use of steam engines for agriculture. Sugar beet was first farmed in 1868, the malting industry was thriving and the Lowestoft fishing industry was at its height at the end of the century.

Up to 1920 Suffolk remained essentially a rural economy. Woodland was farmed or managed. Fields were small and hedges high. Roads were rough and stones, picked from the fields (often by school children) to avoid damage to ploughs, were stacked in piles ready for the village roadman to 'renew' the surface of the local by-ways. Sheep were much more in evidence than they are today, especially on the Sandlings, although with the present restrictions on dairy produce many farms seem to be resorting back to sheep. As late as 1933 there were sixty-four mills in Suffolk, twenty-nine watermills and thirty-five windmills.

And what of today?
The small fields of High Suffolk have, with the destruction of hedges, given way to large areas of arable land. Fishing at Lowestoft has declined to be superseded by the off-shore oil and gas industry. Flour and the production of animal feedstuffs continues to be an important local industry. Nuclear power stations loom over the beach at Sizewell in the same way as the British Telecom Research Station towers over Martlesham Heath and

the hangers of the old wartime aerodrome, itself replaced by a new village and industrial estate. As I write, even the large airbases at Bentwaters and Woodbridge have been closed and their future use remains uncertain. Felixstowe Dock has encroached on the marshland of the River Orwell to become Europe's largest container port, handling well over a million containers a year.

Ipswich's rope making industry of the past has been replaced by the insurance industry. The railways of the Victorian age have either been electrified, converted to diesel, or closed, while the roads, modernised to cope with ever increasing traffic, still traverse the routes of many of the ancient trackways of the past.

THE SUFFOLK COUNTRYSIDE
Its flora and fauna

EXCEPT FOR THE COASTAL BELT which rarely exceeds the 20m contour level, South-Eastern Suffolk is gently undulating and only towards the west around Hadleigh does the land rise above 50m. The area can be divided into three when considering the countryside and its wide diversity of flora and fauna.

The southern part of the county covers the Stour Valley, famous for its associations with Constable and Gainsborough, and included Dedham Vale which is designated an Area of Outstanding Natural Beauty (A.O.N.B.). Also in this part are the valleys of the rivers Gipping, Orwell and Deben, which themselves have areas designated as Sites of Special Scientific Interest (S.S.S.I)

The Suffolk Coastline with its saltmarshes, sand dunes, heathland areas and shingle banks is an A.O.N.B.. The coastline is uniform with few promontories or bays. Between Dunwich and Aldeburgh there are low cliffs of sand or clay, or Norwich crag, and there is also a short stretch of cliff of Red Crag and London Clay near Bawdsey in the south. To the south of Aldeburgh and north of Dunwich the land is very flat and marshy. A fifty mile stretch of the coast from Kessingland in the north to Felixstowe Ferry in the south is designated as a Heritage Coast, one of thirty-seven Heritage Coasts in England and Wales given special protection and management. Perhaps Suffolk's stretch is unique in that, largely because of the number of rivers that drain into the North Sea, there is no coast road to encourage easy access; as a result the area remains relatively un-developed.

Central Suffolk, or High Suffolk as it has been called elsewhere, is a source for many of the rivers (see Map A, Page 8), and is characterised by its rolling landscape, valleys and scattered woodland.

The whole area is studded with reserves both large and small, many managed by the Suffolk Wildlife Trust, and most of these are open to visitors at all times. A list may be found on Page 120 together with details of facilities provided by Suffolk County Council which may be of interest to walkers in the area.

Suffolk enjoys an equable climate which, together with only gently undulating terrain, makes for easy walking. One characteristic which will be met is the strong wind. Cold winds persist in the winter until late in the season and help to retard spring growth. Spring and early summer are usually dry, and indeed daily hours of sunshine are above average. Conversely, winters tend to be colder than in other southern counties. The dryer winds of the summer soon have their effect on the surface land, turning both soil and grass pale. The temperature of the coastal areas is lower as is the rainfall which can be four or five inches less than in the west of the county; the average fall is twenty-two inches, (or 55cms), in the east rising to twenty-seven inches in the west. Indeed in the summer when it is cloudy inland there is often bright sunshine on the coast. Thunder and hail storms can affect particular areas in late summer and autumn originating at the head of river valleys like the Gipping or the Deben. A few areas such as the peninsula between the Deben and the Orwell, where I live, have a lower average rainfall than the rest of the county.

Rivers and Estuaries.
From the north to the south, the area is rich in the birdlife to be found on the estuaries and tidal reaches of Suffolk's rivers. The River Blyth is a good example. Below Blythburgh village is an expanse of tidal mudflats which were formed in the 1920s when the sea wall was breached, and both migratory and resident waders are in abundance. Further south, the River Alde below Snape attracts similar numbers and the S.W.T.'s newly acquired reserve on the Hazelwood marsh will provide another facility for birdwatchers. The increase of avocets in the area since 1950 has been a well documented success story for the R.S.P.B.; indeed, in the last twenty years since I have lived in Suffolk, their numbers have continued to increase and large parties now winter on the Alde.
The Deben, Orwell and Stour too are important sites for large numbers of waders, wildfowl and gulls. Their estuaries and mudflats are home for large flocks of wintering wigeon, shelduck, teal and Brent geese, as well as redshank and dunlin. The threat to these river habitats, arising from recreational use and, in the case of the River Orwell, heavy commercial use, is at present giving cause for concern. The expansion of the dock area at Felixstowe has destroyed a large area of feeding ground for waders, while dredging and the passage of shipping is causing the erosion of mudflats and marsh. The situation is being carefully monitored by conservation bodies. The saltings are colonised by masses of Sea Purslane, Sea Pink, Sea Aster, Scurvy Grass and Glasswort, with the occasional patch of Samphire, a plant once more becoming a delicacy. On the verges of the saltings Sea Plaintain and Club Rush are common. One third of all the saltings in Suffolk are on the River Deben.

Beaches.
The beaches are a mixture of sand and shingle with large banks of shingle

being formed by the North Sea drift of eroded material from cliffs further north. The great Orfordness Spit is a good example (see Page 14). The silting-up of river estuaries is continually changing the coastline and providing habitats for birds and plant life. Landguard Point at Felixstowe, for example, is not only an excellent observation point for migration but a home for Sea Holly, Sea Kale, Yellow Horned Poppy and Stinking Goosefoot amongst others. Shingle banks also provide ideal nesting sites for Little Terns and Ringed Plover - their eggs well camouflaged by the pebbles - and they support butterflies like the Wall Brown and Small Heath. Patches of Marram grass strengthen the dunes at Minsmere.

The erosion caused by the North Sea Drift has completely enclosed some estuaries causing the formation of meres which are good observation points for migratory birds. Benacre Broad in the north of the area is an example.

Heaths.

The coastal region once featured large areas of heathland but house building, airfield construction, forestry and farming have reduced it to several small areas most of which are carefully protected and managed. In sixty years 80% of coastal heath has been destroyed. Loss of heathland is well illustrated at Martlesham. Twenty years ago I was able to wander over the disused airfield, there to find lapwing's nests hidden amongst the tussocky grass. Now this heath and the old runways have disappeared under a new village, and recently the Ministry of Transport have even cut swathes through the gorse bordering the side of a by-pass in deference to the automobile 'god'.

Fortunately the National Trust now has responsibility for a large part of Dunwich Heath and the Suffolk Wildlife Trust for Hollesley Heath and Westleton Heath. Tunstall and Blaxhall Commons are other good heathland areas cared for by local councils. The acid soil provides a different habitat for plant and bird life. At Hollesley the reserve comprises woodland of pine and birch and open expanses of heather. Birdlife includes Crossbill and Siskin, and both the Redstart and Nightjar breed there. Muntjac deer may be observed.

Gorse, ling and bell heathers, the trefoils and red spurrey are typical heathland plants. With the absence of sheep on the heathlands and fewer rabbits than earlier in the century, bracken and birch scrub tend to predominate.

Woods and Forests.

Suffolk, once covered in woodland, is not now a heavily wooded county and remaining areas of woodland are scattered and fairly small. A few examples of ancient woodland exist, notably a Park at Staverton near

Butley. Other woodlands like Martins Wood near Bentley (Walk 18) and Wolves Wood near Hadleigh were well managed and coppiced as part of a thriving industry to provide stakes and fencing. Now they are mixed woods of standard trees and coppiced areas of hazel and chestnut, making an excellent habitat for a variety of woodland birds including the nightingale.

Bluebells proliferate in these and other old woods together with Wood Anemones, Wood Sorrel and Barren Strawberry which are indicators of ancient woodland. These spring flowers flourish in years of light but require years of shade to smother grasses and other plants which might take over. A managed or coppiced woodland is therefore an ideal habitat. Oliver Rackham in his book expalins how, in the past, woods were managed for the production of timber (from standard trees) and wood (from coppicing). Woods are self-renewing and only cease to exist when deliberately destroyed or misused. He writes 'Almost every wood of which the coppice stools remain is worth preserving. Re-coppicing is the best conservation policy as it brings to life the traditional working of the wood'. The alternative is to do nothing. 'Three strands of wire is the simplest conservation measure.'

The 1920s saw a rapid re-afforestation of parts of Suffolk, especially the coastal heathlands, by the Forestry Commission. To travel along the road from Woodbridge to Orford almost gave one the experience of a Scandinavian forest. Until recently planting was almost entirely of conifer which encouraged birs like the siskin and some mammals, especially fallow deer. But their dark canopy denuded the forest floor of plant life. With the storm of 1987 and the destruction of thousands of pines the scenery was changed overnight. At first the torn stumps were reminiscent of a World War 1 scene in Flanders. Now, seven years later, regeneration is at work (in parts not yet replanted) with birch, in particular, replacing the uprooted stumps. It is hoped a policy of mixed plantations will replace the old stands of conifer.

Hedges.

Although Suffolk did not fare so badly as neighbouring Norfolk, miles of hedgerow were lost in the 1960s and 70s with the consequent loss of the wild flowers and other life that they sheltered. Verges of surviving hedges, both in the field and by the roadside, too were sprayed leading to the extinction of many plants. The destruction of hedges had a particular effect on butterflies which research shows use the hedges as thoroughfares. A hedge leading into a wood is particularly good for Orange Tips, the Holly Blue and Commas. Also the decrease of oak trees between the wars depleted some species and the loss of grasslands to the plough led to the decline of the Brown Argus and Dingy Skipper. During this century twenty-one species have become extinct with a decline in seventeen others. Thirteen species, amongst which are Peacocks, Small Skippers, Gatekeepers and Brimstones have have shown little change in numbers, whilst three, the Essex Skipper, White Admiral and Speckled Wood have shown an increase.

A list of species to be seen in the area is included at the end of the book.

Leave livestock, and crops and machinery alone.
Take your litter home.
Help to keep all water clean.
Protect wildlife, plants and trees.
Take special care on country roads.
Make no unnecessary noise.
Enjoy the countryside and respect its life and work.
Guard against all risk of fire.
Fasten all gates.
Keep your dogs under close control.
Keep to public paths across farmland.
Use gates and stiles to cross fences, hedges and walls.

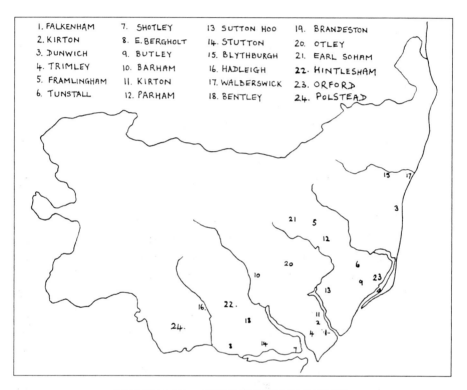

1. FALKENHAM	7. SHOTLEY	13 SUTTON HOO	19. BRANDESTON
2. KIRTON	8. E. BERGHOLT	14. STUTTON	20. OTLEY
3. DUNWICH	9. BUTLEY	15. BLYTHBURGH	21. EARL SOHAM
4. TRIMLEY	10. BARHAM	16. HADLEIGH	22. HINTLESHAM
5. FRAMLINGHAM	11. KIRTON	17. WALBERSWICK	23. ORFORD
6. TUNSTALL	12. PARHAM	18. BENTLEY	24. POLSTEAD

THE WALKS - WITH STARTING POINTS

THE WALKS - in order of difficulty

Kirton Creek

WALK 1: CREEK TO CREEK
Falkenham to Kirton

Start: *Falkenham. Grid Ref: 293391*
O.S.Map: *Landranger 169 or Pathfinder 1054, 1031*
Distance: *5 miles*
Time: *2½ hours*
Parking: *Park near the church or at the head of the track by the telephone box 100m ahead.*

This is an interesting walk across arable and reclaimed marshland and along the river wall visiting both Falkenham and Kirton creeks. A receding tide will give the added interest of wildfowl and waders feeding on the mudflats. This is a walk which really celebrates the beauty of the River Deben. There can be few river scenes more beautiful than the view up-river from Kirton Creek on a frosty winter afternoon or on a sunlit summer's day.

LEAVE FALKENHAM keeping the church on the left and in 50m take the track on the left by the side of the second house. At the first junction bear right along the hedge in the direction of the river and then left to drop down a slight slope.

As the path bears right at the bottom of the slope note the patches of Horsetail on either side. This is one of a group of flowerless and leafless perennials with jointed stems, each joint with its toothed fringe taking the place of leaves. The stems are rather like a natural piece of Lego. I can remember as a child separating the sections and then re-joining them again. The Giant Horsetail grows up to three feet in height and is often found in damp places or where there is a spring.

Follow the path to the river wall and Falkenham Creek keeping the dyke on the right.

The exact age of the turf walls is uncertain. Early in the sixteenth century a levy of 12p an acre was made for the upkeep of the walls and Queen Elizabeth 1 set up a commission to survey the marshes and build new walls. It appears certain that the walls nearer the river mouth were there before 1500. In the fourteenth century the stretch from the estuary up to Kirton was known as the port of Goseford or Gooseford - were geese flocking to the Deben then as now? - a port of more importance then than either Ipswich or Felixstowe. In 1338 Goseford sent fifteen ships and 538 men to France in King Edward's name and as a reward was given the right to supply the port of Calais, then owned by the English, with beer and

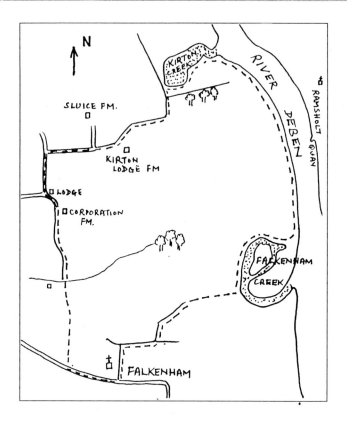

provisions. However, by the time of the Armada in 1586, decline was already setting in as Goseford raised only three ships for the fleet.

The walk continues left along the wall, at first round the creek, and then following the river's edge.

Ramsholt marina on the far side of the river becomes obvious with its public house and, to the left, the round tower of the church. The tower, thought to date from Saxon times, possibly served as a watchtower to guard for marauders entering the estuary. Ramsholt itself used to be much larger and as late as the 1960s several cottages were demolished leaving only the inn. In the past the inn was said to have been a venue for smugglers, and The Dog at Falkenham (now Dog Cottage), with its clear view of Ramsholt, to have received the 'run goods'.

After passing Ramsholt, the wall soon curves left into Kirton Creek.

This was once the busy port of Guston, and ferries ran from here to Ramsholt and Shottisham. In the nineteenth century a brickyard in the nearby fields was perhaps the last chapter in its industrial life. Now only the occasional yachtsman will attempt to launch a boat at high tide, and the remains of an old barge is the only evidence of past commerce. The barge was 'The Three Sisters', at the creek in 1932 to discharge manure. Apparently, she was in such poor order that the crew refused to take her out again and walked home to Ipswich!

Here as on other stretches of the river, shelduck and redshank are common. The shelduck can be distinguished from other duck by its large size and black and white appearance. Closer to, its bright red bill and pink feet are conspicuous as is the knob at the top of the drake's bill. The shelduck is a very sociable bird and is usually seen feeding on the mudflats. It nests further inland, even choosing deserted rabbit holes or bramble bushes in which to brood. Eggs are laid in May and twelve young form the average family. Despite its size the shelduck doesn't venture far out on the water like some ducks.

The redshank is a medium-sized brown wader with, as its name suggests, orange-red legs. When disturbed it has a distinctive erratic flight and a tuneful 'teu-teu' call and, on landing, it briefly holds its wings raised over its back. A white band on the rear of each wing is another conspicuous feature.

At the end of the wall the path follows the fence behind the tall scrub bordering the creek and then turns left up the slope to the trees. Turn right where the tracks meet and walk up to Kirton Lodge Farm. Go between the farm buildings and along a concrete track. Where this meets the metalled lane turn left up the lane as far as the white lodge and continue left after the lodge. Keep straight forward past the farm buildings and eventually descend to a small stream. Carry on up the slope and then between hedges to come to Yew Tree House on the Falkenham road, bearing left for the return to the church.

A look inside St .Ethelbert's Church is well worthwhile. Only eighteen churches are dedicated to St. Ethelbert, a Saxon King of the East Angles murdered by King Offa of Mercia, and nine of these are in Norfolk and four in Suffolk. A church existed here in 1307 although much of the present church dates from the fifteenth and sixteenth centuries. The church has a beautiful tower, and of particular note inside is the single-hammerbeam and arch-braced roof with its carved angels. There is an interesting fifteenth century font with its eight panels depicting emblems of Christ, the four Evangelists and others. These were preserved from the Puritans by a concealing coat of plaster.

WALK 2: FIELD AND FARM
Kirton and Around

Start: *Kirton. Grid Ref: 277397*
O.S.Map *Landranger 169. Pathfinder 1054 & 1031*
Distance: *4 miles*
Time: *1 ½ hours*
Parking: *At Village Green*

> *An easy walk across field and by track, and a short stretch of road with the added interest of a lake.*

THE WALK COMMENCES at the village green. Cross the road in front of the bus shelter and take the track on the left of the hedge by the sign 'Greensleeves'. After crossing two fields a stile is reached. The path continues over the stile to a small stream and a plank bridge.

Cross and bear right up the slope, and then between hedges to come on to a farm track with nearby buildings. Keeping the buildings on your right continue along the track. Ignore the track that goes left and veer slightly right to descend a slope to an old water course.

> On the right look out for apple blossom in the hedgerow, or later in the year the fruit.

After crossing another field a conifer plantation is seen on the left, and by the side of the track is a stretch of overgrown brick and flint wall by the edge of the field, the only remains of some long disused dwellings. The path now becomes sandy and the lake can be seen.

> A footpath recently developed by the Ramblers' Association runs along the northern edge of the lake and this makes an attractive diversion. Water birds to be seen on the lake include coot (with white bills), moorhen (red bills) and tufted duck. The latter can easily be recognised by their white flank contrasting with the rest of the black plumage. As its name suggests the male has a tuft or crest on the back of its head; the female is browner without the tuft.

The walk can be shortened by continuing along this lakeside path to the road, bearing right to walk back to the village. Otherwise retrace your steps and return to the original track and go up the slope to the main road. Here turn left and continue on the road signposted Newbourne, past the kennels. Where the road bends sharp left by the farmhouse, follow the track at the side of the converted barn. Keep on this track dropping down onto a sandy stretch and then up the rise which gives on to a superb view of the River Deben and surrounding countryside.

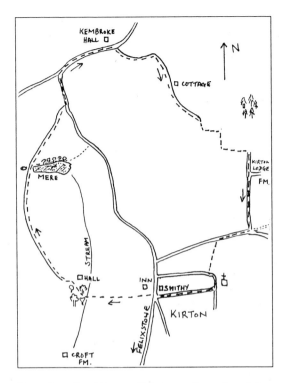

On a clear day it is possible to see four church towers from this ridge and, if the right spot is chosen, even a fifth!

The track continues down a dip and twists round the edge of the field and then up a steepish slope to the hedge at the top. After a stretch between hedges a metalled lane is reached. Bear right and in about 400m turn right at the white lodge. In a short while a footpath goes diagonally left across a field towards Kirton Church.

Kirton Church is dedicated to St. Mary and St. Martin and there has been a church on this site for a thousand years. Domesday Book mentions a rector called Godric who was living here in 1086. There is no trace of the original building and the earliest part is the font which is thought to date from the thirteenth century. The nave and chancel are sixteenth century with later Victorian additions. There is much evidence of a well-cared-for church with pews and kneelers made and donated by parishioners and the entrance gates made by the village blacksmith. A recent addition in 1991 is a beautiful tapestry denoting the many organisations in the village.

With the church on the left bear right at the junction to return to the village green.

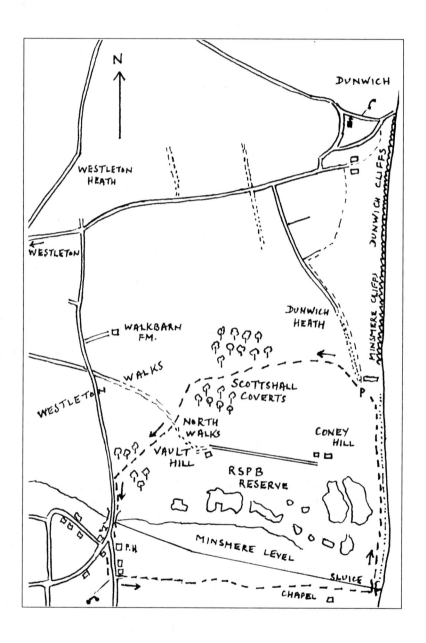

WALK 3: WOODS, MARSH AND SEA
Dunwich, Eastbridge and Minsmere

Start: *Dunwich Heath   Grid Ref: 477678*
O.S.Map: *Landranger 156 .*
Distance: *5 miles, or 9 miles to include Dunwich*
Time: *2½ hours or 5 hours*
Parking: *NT Car Park*
Refreshments: *Take sandwiches unless you relish the idea of fish and chips at Dunwich (last orders 4.00pm). For a brief rest and drink there is The Eel's Foot at Eastbridge.*

For variety and changing scenery this walk can hardly be bettered. Beginning first across heather the path rapidly descends into woodland, and then across arable fields to meet marshland and the tiny village of Eastbridge. More fields lead to the dunes and beach bordering Minsmere and thence into Dunwich with its rich history.

FACING THE PUBLIC convenience, take the path to the right which runs parallel to the NT road and in about 100m turn left at the coastal path sign. The coastguard cottages are now behind you. In 200m, on meeting a low barrier, bear left and take the path which descends the hill. At the first Dunwich Heath sign bear right and keep the stream on your left. Continue until the next NT Dunwich Heath sign appears and, ignoring the arrow pointing right, bear left over the stile.

Notice that the woodland, at first mainly bracken and birch, changes for a short while to heather and then to mixed woodland including sweet chestnut. Here the path passes much evidence of natural decay with rotting tree trunks, attractive fungi in the autumn, the sound of the woodpecker and, in summer, the whitethroat.

At the next junction turn left. The path then follows along beside a brushwood barrier which forms the boundary of Scottshall Coverts. On meeting a lane, cross straight over to a grassy track with a view of Sizewell Power Station to the left and then through a second wood. At the second Minsmere Reserve sign bear right on the tarmac road edged with lime trees, past the main entrance to the Reserve and continue along to a bridge.

Here in summer the stream is covered with yellow water lily, or 'brandy bottle' as it is sometimes called because of the smell it gives of stale alcohol. Covering the banks are the large leaves of butterbur. Possibly used in the past for wrapping butter, the latin name for this plant means broad-brimmed hat and John Gerard, the Elizabethan herbalist wrote that 'the leafe is bigge and large inough to keepe a man's head from raine and from the heat of the sunne'. Powder made from the roots of the plant was used in the Middle Ages to remove spots from the skin.

At the road junction take the left fork past the Eel's Foot public house. By Rose Cottage turn left at the sign, Minsmere Sluice, and in 50m sharp right down a narrow track (FP). At the stile continue to follow the signs to the Sluice.

On the way across towards the beach note a 'tacky screen' erected by Nuclear Electric to monitor atmospheric pollution. The amount of radiation in the dust which collects on the screen is measured to ensure that minimum levels are maintained.

Proximity to Minsmere R.S.P.B. Reserve will bring rewards to the keen birdwatcher, and on this part of the walk they may include a sight of the Marsh Harrier which hunts over the fields and marshland to the left. Frequently they indulge in aerial displays over the marsh between the path and the trees of the reserve, and a careful watch on the bushes in front of the rise may reveal a bird perching or gliding from bush to bush. The Marsh Harrier is the largest of the European harriers, heavily built with broad wings. The adult female has dark plumage with a creamy yellow head whilst the male looks lighter in flight with its grey wings and tail.

The path passes near the ruins of an old chapel to arrive at the Sluice. Now there is a bracing walk left along by the dunes or on the beach with an opportunity to visit one of the hides open to the public.

Depending on the time of year a wide variety of bird life can be seen feeding and nesting. Minsmere is famous for the avocet, but terns, godwit and ruff are just some of the long list to be sighted on a summer's day on the reserve. In the winter, geese and many varieties of duck take their place. Don't miss a wander along the shingle beach but beware of restricted areas in the breeding season which protect the nesting sites of the little tern.

Arriving at Minsmere cliffs the walk can be shortened here by climbing the wooden steps which give on to the car park and the starting point.

It was on these cliffs that one of many beacons was lit to warn of the approach of the Spanish Armada in 1588.

If time and energy allow continue along the beach to visit the village of Dunwich.

Halfway, watch out for the sand martins nests high up on the cliffs. Fishing boats drawn up on the beach soon indicate the edge of the village, once, in the Middle Ages, a town extending seawards. The See of East Anglia was founded here in AD 632 and by Domesday the town had a population of

Dunwich Cliffs

over five hundred and already boasted three churches. In the thirteenth century it was a thriving port with over eighty ships, but prevailing tides led to the silting up of the natural harbour formed from old river outlets and trade transfered to other ports such as Ipswich. Violent storms, particularly in the fourteenth and eighteenth centuries led to the final destruction of what had been an important town.

Turn left past the fishermen's huts and the cafe where excellent fish and chips are sold, and continue up the road to a little triangle. To the right lie the Church and a Museum. The route takes the left fork, and in about 50m turn left up a footpath which is soon signed the coast path.

This passes what remains of the Franciscan Friary of Greyfriars, rebuilt with the permission of Edward 1 in 1289. (The first Greyfriars of 1277 had been built too close to the sea). It was suppressed along with other monastic buildings in 1538 and rapidly became a ruin. Now only the west gate, refectory and precinct walls remain. The nearby church of All Saints was the last of the nine medieval churches of Dunwich to succomb to the sea, its tower finally disappearing in 1919.

At Friars House continue forward at the road and in 100m turn left down the footpath signposted Minsmere Road. The path soon wends through a pleasant wood to meet the road which leads left to return to the NT car park.
Before leaving you may wish to visit the Information Centre which has an interesting display on the locality.

47

WALK 4: FIELD AND RIVERSIDE RESERVE
Trimley and the River Orwell

Start: *Falkenham   Grid Ref: 293390*
O.S.Map: *Landranger 169 Pathfinder 1054*
Distance: *9 miles*
Time: *4 hours plus any time for birdwatching*
Parking: *By the church, or at the head of the track on the left 100m down the lane.*

Although this is a longer walk there is an opportunity for a break and some rewarding birdwatching at the hafway point. The first stage is mainly across fields by lane and track eventually to arrive at Trimley foreshore and the reserve owned by the Suffolk Wildlife Trust. The walk continues along the river wall and returns to the start point by field and track.

WITH THE CHURCH on the left follow the lane down the slope and continue up the other side of the dip known as Falkenham Sink.

At the top there are extensive views across farmland to the estuary of the River Deben at Felixstowe Ferry. The radio mast at Bawdsey, the centre for radar research in the early stages of World War 11 can be seen, as well as two reminders of an earlier war against Napoleon in the shape of Martello towers. These are two towers out of a total of seventy-four which were built from 1803 to 1812 along the Channel and East Coast as a defence against threatened invasion. The towers are 30 - 40 feet high, elliptical in shape, with walls up to nine feet thick on the seaward side and, when built, were often surrounded by a ditch. Entry was gained by a door twenty feet above ground level to the magazine and the living quarters below. A platform on top of the tower held a howitzer and swivel gun. The name Martello is possibly derived from Cape Mortello in Corsica where, in 1794, a similar tower proved very difficult to capture during the Peninsula War. Each tower took about 700,000 bricks to build and the yellow bricks used came from London by barge and were probably unloaded on the beach.

Go as far as the junction with a lane to Deben Lodge Farm and continue in the same direction along the footpath (Y.W.M.) on the right opposite a farm cottage. After crossing two fields descend a shallow valley to Falkenham Brook. Pass over a stile and cross three more fields. Bear right across the third field to a gate and stile. Then aim left of the two oaks in the middle of the next field for a stile in the hedge. Cross the stile to enter a narrow copse.

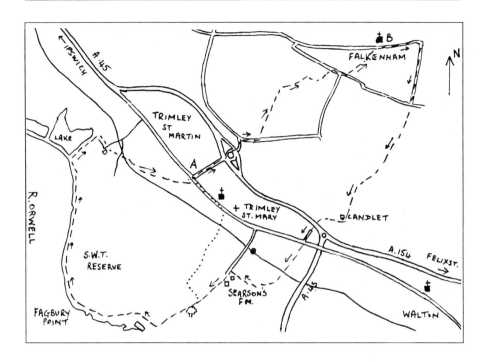

In the Autumn this area is a fertile feeding ground for finches, especially goldfinch which feed off the seedheads of thistle, cow parsley and other weeds. The goldfinch is easily distinguished from other finches by its black wings with a band of brilliant yellow, and its red, white and black face. They have the usual bouncy finch flight but with a lighter and more dancing action. It has a liquid 'switt, switt' call.

Continue through the copse and across the next field to follow the hedge left of Candlet Farmhouse to meet a gravelled track. Turn right, and in about 300m bear left across a field (the line is marked by a row of four oak trees) to meet the A45 near a roundabout. The dual carriageway should be crossed WITH GREAT CARE. ALLOW FOR THE SPEED OF TRAFFIC AND WAIT FOR A GOOD SPACE BEFORE CROSSING. Descend the embankment, cross the central reservation and go through the screen of trees.
A stile may be observed on the far side which gives on to a residential cul-de-sac. Go straight forward and cross the old High Street at the end to a stile opposite. Continue forward keeping the hedge on the left. Go under the railway bridge and then bear sharp right to go under a second railway culvert. In 100m, go left along the top of a bank to meet a gravel track which leads up to the farm.

Here you may well be welcomed by raucous cries from the rookery in the trees on the right. Rooks, which may be distinguished from crows by the bare patch on the face and the shaggy feathering around their legs, are very gregarious. They start nesting in late March usually in the upper branches of trees and often in a previous year's nest. In autumn and winter the rookery is used as a roosting place.

At the farm follow the sign to the Nature Reserve and Fagbury Point. Nearing the large storage warehouse (which will soon be screened by trees) the path forks. An interesting detour may be made to Fagbury Point to watch the hive of activity at the container port. Otherwise bear right to the reserve which is owned by the Suffolk Wildlife Trust.

There are four hides overlooking different aspects of the marshland and the various pools which attract a wide variety of waders, wildfowl and other birds. The hides are open at all times to visitors but please ensure that flaps and doors are closed before leaving. An interesting Visitor Centre is open at certain times during the week.

Continue along the river wall and at the point where the river bends to the left the track swings away from the wall up the slope towards Loompit Lake. Bear right away from the lake towards a farm. After passing a pink-washed house turn right along the metalled road, and where the road bends sharp left, take the footpath between two houses to cross a field. Follow the line of the telegraph poles towards the corner of the field, cross the lane and continue to the stile over the railway.

Cross with care and follow the path round the field, keeping the hedge on your left, and aim for the gap between the houses. This gives on to a roundabout. Take the second exit and in about 200m cross the A45 slip roads by the left bridge and follow the road to Kirton. A little further on turn right down the lane (s.p.Falkenham) and in a few yards turn left down a bridleway. In about a quarter of a mile turn right and continue along the track until a lane is reached. Almost opposite is a footpath and entrance to a riding stable. Follow the path to the left of the white building, Swiss Farm, and then, at the road, go right to return to Falkenham Church.

WALK 5: CASTLE, FIELD AND CHURCH
Framlingham to Dennington

Start: *Framlingham Castle. Grid Ref: 286636*
O.S.Map: *Landranger 156.*
Distance: *5 miles*
Time: *3 hours*
Parking: *Castle car park (if visiting the castle). Market Square or by the church.*
Refreshments: *The Queens Head, Dennington. The Castle Inn or Teapots & Quails, Framlingham.*

> *Although the majority of this walk consists of fieldwork there is much that is unexpected, and with the castle, a moated house and a beautiful church en route, a lot to interest and remember. Dennington Church is one of the most interesting in the area.*

START FROM THE CASTLE car park and walk towards the castle. Pass through the turnstile on the left before the drawbridge and over the little bridge crossing the ditch to bear left on the path round what was once the moat. The mere and the grounds of Framlingham College soon become visible. The path continues down some steps over a second bridge and straight on. After passing the wicket gate bear left. Go over a stile and plank bridge and follow the Y.W.M sign round the edge of the College playing field keeping the stream on the right.

On reaching a lane go left for about 200m and turn right on the footpath just past the farm. Go diagonally across the field aiming for the oak tree to the left of the grey barn. Keeping on the left side of the barn, drop down the slope and through the hedge to the track between two farm buildings. Here turn left to cross the field with the hedge and stream on the right. Continue forward over the stile ignoring the footpath to the right to arrive at the B1116 road.

> During winter, whilst crossing these fields, you may disturb a hare. Unlike the rabbit, there are three species of hare to be found in the British Isles, the brown, the blue and the Irish, the latter being restricted to Ireland and the blue to the mountains of Scotland. The brown hare is found all over Great Britain and is common wherever there is cultivation. It may be distinguished from the rabbit only by its greater size, black ear-tips and black upper tail. Sometimes they assume a more greyish appearance in winter. Hares do most of their feeding at night, lying up in their 'forms' by day.

At the road turn left and then almost immediately right to continue on a path (Y.W.M) round the field edge. In a short while a ridge-like mound may be seen on the left. Just past this go right, through a gap in the hedge marked by a pollarded

beech tree and underfoot a brick-lined but turf-covered bridge. Turn right to follow the ditch and then left round the field towards a copse. Keeping this on the right, continue forward until a track is reached by the side of some farm buildings. Stay on the track bearing right and at the cross tracks keep straight on by the side of a tall hawthorn hedge bordering the ditch. At the end of the hedge turn right and aim towards the church tower and the black barns. Beyond the barns lies the road leading to Dennington Church.

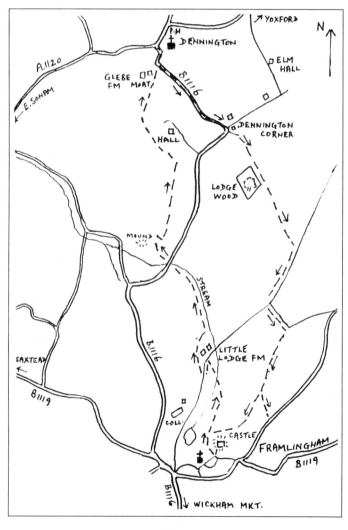

The church of St. Mary's is well worth a visit for its wealth of interesting treasures. The parclose screens surrounding the two side chapels, one of which commemorates William Lord Bardolph who fought at Agincourt and later served as Chamberlain to Henry V1, the three-deck pulpit and the beautiful carvings on the benches are just a few of the things to attract interest. Amongst the carvings depicting animals and creatures from mythology look for the pelican, the mermaid and the only example in an English church of a Sciapod, a strange creature resting under the shade of his huge foot.

From Dennington retrace your steps along the B1116 road (s.p.Framlingham) and in about one mile, where the road bends sharp right, go straight forward to follow a footpath that leaves the road on the left by the side of a cottage. Cross the ditch at the end of the first field through a gap in the hedge and then aim across the next field for the left side of Lodge Wood opposite. A detour round this field may be necessary if a crop is growing. Continue forward on the path by the wood to meet a metalled lane. Turn right down a slope for about 400m to take a left turn up to Great Lodge Farm. At the top of the rise bear right on a W.M. path leading back towards the castle. At the bottom of the incline cross a plank bridge and then a choice of paths leads back either up the slope to the N.E. side of the town or right to rejoin the path by the side of the castle.

The castle was developed by the Bigod family in the twelfth century although there was an earlier fortification here in Saxon times. The castle is interesting because, unlike its nearest neighbour at Orford and other Norman forts, it was built on the lines of the Saracen castles with a long curtain outer wall interspersed with thirteen towers. Stone for its building came from Barnack in Northamptonshire and was transported by sea. The mere to the west of the castle is partly artificial since, in the earlier construction of the mound, a man-made ditch or moat would have been formed of which the present mere is a part.

The building has had a chequered history. The Bigods fell into disgrace and the castle was forfeited to the king and later it was possessed by the Mowbray family. Late in Elizabeth's reign it became a prison and subsequently it was converted into a poorhouse. Perhaps one of the more colourful events surrounding the castle was when Queen Mary raised her standard here in 1552 against the forces supporting Lady Jane Grey. Thirteen thousand armed men were recruited from the surrounding countryside.

Although much of the castle was later demolished, some of it reportedly for road-making, it is worth a visit and a dizzying walk round the top of the wall may be made to enjoy the views.

WALK 6:   FOREST, HEATH AND RIVER
Tunstall, Iken and Snape

Start;   *Tunstall. Grid Ref: 374549*
O.S.Map: *Landranger 156. Pathfinder 1009*
Distance: *6½ miles*
Time: *4 hours*
Parking: *At Tunstall Common at the beginning of the track marked by post number 15*
Refreshments: *Tea Rooms at Snape Maltings or the Plough & Sail Inn.*

> *A delightful and varied walk through forest, across heath and common land and along the River Alde. Although the storm of 1987 decimated the Tunstall Forest there are signs of re-birth.*

START FROM TUNSTALL COMMON by taking the track which leaves from the B1078 road at right angles and head east crossing heather-covered common.

> Much of the land either side of the track was forest destroyed by the hurricane of 1987 and there are a few clumps of tall trees which survive as a reminder. Large areas of the neighbouring Rendlesham Forest were also destroyed and parts still have to be cleared of debris.

Pass two cottages and soon the River Alde comes into view.

> Iken Church tower is visible and the large red building in the distance is Black Heath House on the far bank of the Alde. The wood surrounding the house is crossed by an old track called Sailor's Path. This was used by fishermen who worked from Aldeburgh and managed to combine that with work at Snape Maltings, an earlier form of 'moonlighting' perhaps!

Cross the road to continue in the same direction by the footpath opposite, keeping the plantation on the left, and follow this to the corner. Here turn right and follow the line of trees until the path bears left along the edge of Oak Covert wood. Keep this wood on the right until meeting a farm track at the corner of the wood. Turn left along the farm track and left again at the metalled lane past a thatched cottage. Continue along the lane to the road junction. Turn right and in 200m take the footpath on the left to Snape.
The path now follows the edge of the mudflats, crossing at one point a small stretch of sandy beach - a good place for a break and a chance to watch the varied bird life.

> Even in winter it is possible at low tide to see small flocks of Avocet waiting for the water to recede enough for them to sift the surface of the mud with their upturned bills for the tiny shrimp-like creatures on which they rely. The Avocet has pied white and black plumage, black bill and blue-grey, stilt-like legs. They walk through the shallow water sweeping their bills

from side to side for food which they swallow with a short upward flip of the head. When resting they will often stand on one leg.

Continue along the edge past some boat houses to meet a small cottage. Go up the path by the cottage, bear right and take the way-marked path to Snape. Cross the field (crowded in summer with parked cars) close to the hedge and continue along the path which in parts is made of railway sleepers raised above the level of the mud. Snape Maltings and the Concert Hall soon come into view.

Before reaching the road the path passes extensive reed beds and then a line of beech trees edged with hawthorn bushes. Here, in early winter, you may be fortunate to see Fieldfares feeding on the berries.

At the road a short detour may be made to visit the Maltings and the various craft centres and galleries which now occupy part of the old buildings. The original buildings of red and yellow brick and white weatherboarding were erected in the mid-nineteenth century for Newson Garrett, the father of Elizabeth Barrett Anderson. The maltings were converted into a concert hall in 1966 which was destroyed by fire two years later. The restoration, maintaining the character of the original maltings, was completed in 1970. The concert hall itself is not usually open except

Tunstall Forest - after the hurricane

55

for concert-goers but sometimes rehearsals and practice classes may be heard in the area behind the hall. Occasionally a sailing barge is moored by the quay and there is a rewarding view down-river across the reed beds and saltings.

If not visiting the Maltings, cross the road and continue ahead on the road signposted Blaxhall, bearing right at the junction. In about half a mile, just after the Blaxhall village sign, turn left onto a path marked by a Forestry post No 14. The path leaves the road opposite a junction with a narrow lane and crosses Blaxhall Common.

The Common is managed by the local parish with the assistance of the Suffolk Trust for Nature Conservation.

In about 15m take the path on the left and follow this for 200m or so to where a number of low posts are set in the ground across a gap on the right. Turn right here and drop down into a small sandy dell and up the other side. Continue forward to arrive at another row of low posts and the Blaxhall Common sign. In a few metres bear left along a red gravel track which borders the edge of the western side of Tunstall Forest. In a short while the B1069 from Tunstall to Snape is reached at a junction with a by-road to Iken. Veer slightly right and cross the B1069 to the track opposite. This wends its way between fields back to the edge of Tunstall Common and the start point by Post 13.

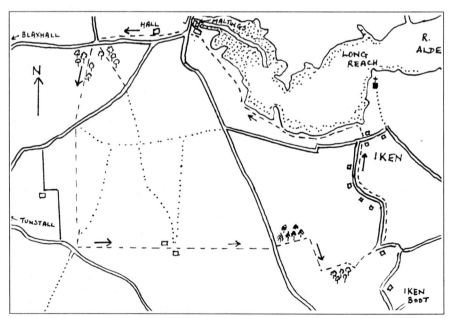

56

WALK 7:   THE TWO RIVERS WALK
Shotley to Erwarton

Start; *Shotley Gate. Grid Ref: 247336*
O.S.Map: *Landranger 169. Pathfinder 1054*
Distance: *6 miles or 8 miles*
Time: *3½ or 4½ hours*
Parking: *On the foreshore near Shotley Pier*
Refreshments: *The Bristol Arms or The Queens Head, Erwarton.*

This varied walk takes in both the River Orwell and the River Stour together with the interesting hamlet of Erwarton. The beginning and final parts of the walk are along river banks with rewarding sights of many wildfowl and waders.

Shotley is in a fine position overlooking both the Orwell, the Stour and the bustling activity of the ports of Felixstowe and Harwich. Shotley itself was noted for being the home of H.M.S. Ganges, a naval cadet training establishment, the buildings of which lie just inland at the start of the walk. This is now closed but the tall mast up which the cadets swarmed remains as a reminder.

LEAVE THE HARBOUR area with the 'Bristol Arms' on the left and follow the road round by the sea wall towards the Marina. Go through the Marina area keeping on the landward side and this eventually leads on to the turf bank of the river wall.

Across the river lies the much extended Port of Felixstowe with its cranes and container yards. In contrast, bordering the river to the north of the docks is a newly developed nature reserve on the Trimley marshes which provides a resting place for many wild birds. Opened in 1992, the reserve is already a haven for many species of birds in both summer and winter.

Continue along the wall passing a tall black and white marker post where the wall curves in a large arc to round the saltings and mudflats of Crane's Hill creek. The hill to the left stretches up to Shotley Church.
(Here there is an opportunity to take a footpath to the left, if a shorter version of the walk is desired. The path joins a lane leading up to the church. Continue along the lane in the same direction past the church and the naval cemetery until Shotley Hall is reached. From this point follow the directions from the * in the main walk description.)

In the winter you may be lucky to see large flocks of Brent geese by the river or the adjacent fields. A flock of three hundred wheeled overhead the last time that I went on this walk. It is a soul-stirring sight as they form and re-form in the air all the while emitting their gurgle-like bark. (For identification details see Walk 14)

Otherwise carry on along the wall rounding Collimer Point where the river bends to the left.

On the other side of the river at this point are Stratton Cliff and the Levington marina. Levington Creek itself and the church can be seen well to the left.

Along this stretch are many marker buoys and posts, and often cormorants may be seen using them as a resting place. The cormorant is a large, long-necked bird with a fairly long bill which is hooked at the tip. Its plumage is a glossy bluish-black and it has a distinguishing white face patch. If disturbed they will fly off low over the water. They feed mainly on eels and

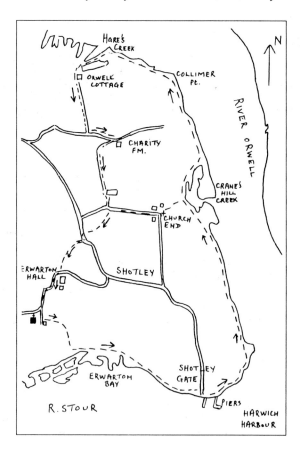

Old Dock - The River Orwell

fish caught whilst submerged under water and so they may often be seen perched with their wings outspread to dry in the wind. If they are seen on the water it can be interesting to time the length of their dives.

The wall eventually reaches Hare's Creek with its saltings. The Orwell Bridge may be seen in the distance. Almost exactly in line with Levington Church, and at the side of a gully lined by the posts of an old pier, a track may be found which leads forward away from the wall and up towards a cottage. Go past the cottage and bear left at the first junction along the metalled lane which descends into a shallow valley before rising up to Charity Farm.
Take the path which bears right at the side of No.1, Charity Farm and past some piggeries.

Glance back towards the river at this point and on the far side can be seen the green cupola of the Observatory at Orwell Park House. Built in 1770, this was the home of Admiral Vernon who captured Portobello in 1739 during the war with Spain. The observatory was added a hundred years later. Vernon is also notable for being the first to issue rum and water to the sailors. It became known as 'grog' after his nickname.

Bear left towards Shotley Hall Farm. Keep the farm buildings on your left and go to the road.
* (The shorter version of the walk rejoins here)
From the farm turn right and follow the lane as far as the main road. Here turn left and in a short while turn right down a lane signed Erwarton Walk. Follow this lane to come to Erwarton Hall.

> The Hall is a large Tudor building rebuilt in 1575 by Sir Philip Parker and was one of the first brick-built stately homes in the country. The previous mansion was owned by Sir Philip Calthorpe whose wife was an aunt of Anne Boleyn. King Henry Vlll was supposed to have courted her here whilst visiting the area on a hunting expedition, and legend says that her heart was buried in a casket in the walls of the nearby church. Much later a casket was discovered in the course of some building work and this was placed in a vault beneath the present organ. In front of the Hall is a fine Elizabethan gatehouse dating from 1549. Built of brick, like the Hall, the tunnel-vaulted arch looks through to the entrance of the house and the gate is capped with nine round pinnacles.

Follow the lane to the right of the Hall to reach the Church.

> St. Mary's is a small church but one with a fine clerestory giving it the feel of a much larger building. Inside, the tomb of the Davillers is interesting for its effigy of a cross-legged knight of the thirteenth century.

Take the track on the left of the churchyard and follow the signed path which leads across a paddock and soon bears right to the wall of the River Stour. Turn left along the wall towards Shotley.

> The mudflats and creeks of Erwarton Bay are feeding areas for many wildfowl such as wigeon and shelduck, and waders which include redshank, oystercatchers, grey plover and godwits.

At a point where the path ascends a rise, an alternative route drops down to the beach, (negotiable at times other than at high tide), to make the final part of the walk more interesting than the route through the housing estate at the top of the rise.

> Back at Shotley you may well be welcomed by the sun shining on the surrounding harbours and agree with the poet Drayton who in 1613 wrote:
>
> > "Besides of all the Roads and Havens of the East
> > This Harbour where they meet is reckoned for the best."

WALK 8: IN THE STEPS OF JOHN CONSTABLE
East Bergholt and Dedhan

Start: *East Bergholt. Grid Ref: 069347*
O.S.Map: *Landranger 169, 168 (Unfortunately, the area of this walk is covered in the corners of these two maps). Pathfinder 1053.*
Distance: *5 miles*
Time: *2 hours (plus, of course, time to appreciate the buildings and views of the area.*
Parking: *The car park at East Bergholt.*
Refreshments: *At Dedham, Flatford or East Bergholt.*

> *This is an easy walk with opportunity to appreciate both the countryside and the three villages visited. Dedham Vale, over which the route goes, is renowned for its beauty, and the walk provides the chance to look at Flatford Mill, two beautiful churches and many attractive houses.*

START FROM EAST BERGHOLT car park by turning right past the Red Lion.

Adjacent to the nearby Post Office is the small cottage with a mansard roof which was Constable's studio early in his career in 1802.

Cross the road and continue forward as far as the memorial cross by the church.

As you go, notice the plaque on the railings which marks the site of the house owned by the Constable family, now replaced by a more modern building. Only the stable block and an entrance gate remain, but the small shop by the gate was where John Dunthorne, a plumber lived. He it was who helped Constable in his early days as a painter, especially in the making of his paints. The church is well worth a visit and there are brief notes at the end of this account.

At the cross follow the lane on the right and in a short while continue right down a track signposted Dedham.

This was most probably the way young John Constable went to school when he was living in East Bergholt. Just after the two cottages is a view on the left which he later used in his painting of The Cornfield.

The track goes over Fen Bridge and in a few metres you bear right to take the path that runs parallel to the track on the other side of the hedge.

You will soon notice that the path is a few feet above the level of the meadows on either side. This was originally constructed on account of the low-lying land and the frequent flooding of the River Stour in the winter, which would otherwise have made this direct route to Dedham impassable.

This is an old path and hedgerow and you may like to test Hooper's Rule, the rough guide to the age of a hedgerow, by counting the number of different species of tree and shrub in any 30 metre stretch. For example, if three different shrubs or trees can be counted, an approximate age of three hundred years may be assumed.

Cross the stile at the end and go forward in the direction of the bank of the River Stour. Turn right and go along the bank until the road is reached by another stile. Several Alder trees grow along the river's edge here. (see Walk 10 for details).

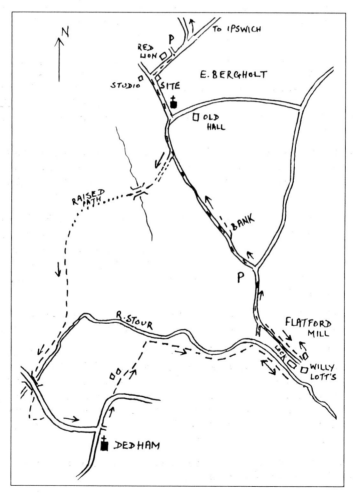

Go left across the bridge and cross the stile to the meadow below. In 50 metres, by the river's edge, there is a stile which allows access to a walkway over the lock gates and a view of the old mill pond.

> Dedham Mill was the subject of one of Constable's paintings, and although the mill has now been converted into flats, some similarities of the view from the water meadow may still be seen.

After crossing the second lock proceed to the road and then turn right into Dedham. At the junction with the high street the route goes left.

> An interesting time may be spent looking at the church and some of the houses. The old grammar school, at which the young John Constable spent some years, is situated just to the left of the church.

Go forward past the church to where the high street curves to the right and take the footpath on the left which cuts diagonally across the field towards some farm buildings. The Old Hall at East Bergholt may be seen on the skyline ahead. Continue on across two stiles towards the river bank. Cross the double stile on the right and follow the line of the willow-lined river and the well marked path to Flatford Mill.

At Flatford a detour may be made along the bank before crossing the bridge to view the old dock where lighters were built or repaired (to be seen on the opposite bank beside the present tea room), the recently restored lock and the Mill House, all of which Constable painted.

> A friend of John Constable, writing his memoirs, said, "We found that the scenery of eight or ten of our late friend's most important subjects might be enclosed by a circle of a few hundred yards at Flatford". (From the National Trust at Bridge Cottage it is possible to buy a wallet containing eight postcards of the artist's paintings, and it is absorbing to compare these views with what can be seen today).

Returning to cross the bridge, a short walk to the right leads past the dry dock down to the fifteenth century Valley Farm on the left and Willy Lott's cottage ahead.

> The Lotts owned several farms in the area, although the real name for the cottage which has achieved fame because of Constable's painting The Haywain, is Gibbons Farm. The cottage and the Mill are a centre for the Field Studies Council and are not open to the public. In the eighteenth century the Mill was owned by Constable's parents, Golding and Ann, and their tomb as well as that of William Lott and John Dunthorne may be seen in East Bergholt churchyard.

Retrace your steps towards the bridge and continue up the lane past the little kiosk to the top of the hill and the car park.

63

Bell Cage,
East Bergholt Church

Go past the car park up the lane and in a short while, by the side of a small brook, leave the lane to walk along the top of the bank on the right.

As the path nears the crest of the rise there is a good view across the Vale to Dedham Church which provided the scene for another of Constable's paintings.

Continue up the lane to return to East Bergholt, the signposted path to Dedham bearing left from the lane before reaching the village.

East Bergholt, in Old English means either a wooded hill or birch grove. It was recorded as a royal manor in the Domesday Book and, like many market towns in Suffolk, flourished from the cloth trade. The decline of this trade may be the reason why the church does not have a completed tower. Bequests made in the middle of the sixteenth century for the building of a steeple obviously did not prove sufficient despite the rumoured promise of some help from Cardinal Wolsey. Another story is that the Devil cast down nightly the work of the builders. The absence of a tower accounts for the existence of a bell cage originally constructed in 1531 at the side of the church. East Bergholt's cage is the only place where the bells are rung by hand without the aid of a rope or wheel.
Amongst many interesting things in the church is a copy of the entry of John Constable in the church's birth register.

WALK 9: IN THE STEPS OF THE MONKS
Butley and Hollesley

Start: *Butley Low Corner. Grid Ref: 382498*
O.S.Map: *Landranger 169. Pathfinder 1031.*
Distance: *10 miles*
Time: *4 ½ hours*
Parking: *Opposite cottages on right.*
Refreshments: *Packed lunch advisable.*

This walk begins in the unspoilt and beautiful area of the Butley river, continues along the banks of the River Ore and then wends back across farmland and the edge of woodland. The early part of the walk not only gives an opportunity to relive some early mediaeval history but also crosses a small R.S.P.B. reserve.

Butley Low and High Corners are a mile or more from the village of Butley and probably owe their situation to the existence of the nearby mediaeval Priory which owned all the surrounding land.

START BY TURNING right at the end of the road down a wide track which leads towards a wood. Continue on keeping the wood on the left and after crossing a stile, head towards Burrow Hill ahead. The path goes diagonally right across the hill to a stile and then descends to another stile to lead to the river bank.

Burrow Hill, with its views across the surrounding countryside and out towards the sea, was ideal for a settlement by man in pre-Roman times, but so far evidence has been found to confirm only a Saxon settlement. However, walkers may not be able to suppress a slight tingle in the spine as they cross today and remember that this lonely place may have been inhabited all those years ago. Then, when there were no walls to retain the waterways, the hill would almost certainly have been an island . Later, invaders like the Angles and Saxons would have ventured further up river to clear forest and make settlements further inland.

On reaching the river wall turn right, and after crossing some stiles, continue forward through the Reserve. From here the view looking up-river with Gedgrave cliff on the far side can hardly be excelled.

Butley Priory was established in 1171 by Ralph de Glanville, Chief Justice of England, and it is absorbing to try to imagine life then in the area. The long spit of Orfordness did not extend this far and it would have been a battle against the sea to build lasting walls and reclaim the land. But by the time the Priory was dissolved in the mid sixteenth century it had become rich with many servants and workers, three of whom were shepherds, so perhaps flocks of sheep were to be seen grazing by the river.

The walk continues along the wall, past a small jetty, and then borders the Lower Gull with the southern end of Havergate Island opposite.

There are views of Orford Castle and Church to the north. Havergate became famous as a breeding ground for the Avocet and now, even in winter, one or two may be seen on the saltings.

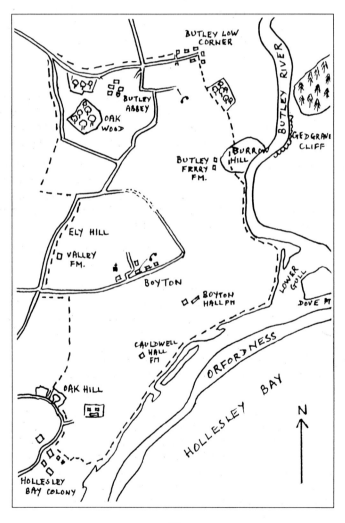

From Lower Gull and opposite Dove Point on Havergate the wall then runs alongside the River Ore, and Orfordness forms the only barrier to the sea
After passing a patch of gorse bushes and a small grove of spruce, the turf wall eventually meets a concrete wall and a wartime pillbox. Here, follow the track which bends to the right to meet the road at Hollesley Bay Colony.

> This seems to be a good area for curlew. During a walk in January, several were to be seen feeding on the mud facing the pillbox and yet more in the fields to the right of the track. A curlew is easy to recognise with its long curved bill and its slow call of 'croo-lee'. It has streaky brown plumage and a swift flight, often gliding for a distance before it lands to feed. It is more easily disturbed than many waders. Females may be distinguished from males by their longer bill.
> Whimbrels, with which curlews can be confused, are smaller birds with a distinctive stripe on their head.
> The route now passes through part of Hollesley Bay Colony. The original purpose of the Colony was to train young farmers who often then went to farm in the British Colonies. Later it was a re-habilitation centre for the unemployed. Since 1938 it has been an 'open' prison for young offenders.

At the road turn right up the hill past the houses built for staff at the Colony and, just past the postbox, take the track on the right that leaves the road by the bus shelter. At the open gateway continue forward keeping the break of conifers on your right, eventually to meet the road at Boyton. Here turn left and then right at the crossroads to go past a farm and up Ely Hill.

> In the Middle Ages, the abbey at Ely owned much of the land in the area and this name probably derives from this period.

Continue along the road until it bends sharply right. Follow the track here that leads left away from the road towards the edge of what forest survived the 1987 storm. (Available maps have the original forest marked in full). The track turns right and in a short while joins a lane. Go forward along the lane past Oak Wood on the right, past a cottage where the road bisects a well stocked duck pond, and up the slope to the road junction Here turn right past some majestic beech trees and continue forward over the crossroads to Butley Low Corner.

> The road passes the site of the old Butley Priory and the surviving gatehouse which was converted into a house in the eighteenth century. It is a beautiful example of flushwork, common to many Suffolk churches. Dressed stone, which in this case came from the area of the River Seine, is combined with knapped flint to make interesting and intricate patterns. Chronicles of the old Priory make it sound at times like a hunting box. The Prior had managed to purchase the nearby Staverton Forest for £240 and in 1516, Mary Tudor, sister of Henry V111, together with the Duke of

Suffolk, Charles Brandon, stayed for a while to hunt and, on occasions, to picnic in Brother Nicholas's garden. They were obviously well entertained as return visits were made. In 1528 the monks took the Queen of France for a 'picnic under the oaks with fun and games'. Records show that the Abbey employed many servants including a warrener, cooks, bakers, maltsters, a cooper and a keeper of 'swannys and pullein'.

Butley Priory

10: GIPPING VALLEY & WOODLAND PATHS
Barham to Coddenham

Start: *Barham, Nr. Claydon, Ipswich Grid Ref: 124512*
O.S.Map: *Landranger 155, 156. Pathfinder 1007*
Distance: *7½ miles*
Time: *4 hours*
Parking: *Barham Picnic Site, accessible from Claydon.*
Refreshments: *The Duke's Head, Coddenham.*

A most interesting walk to be enjoyed during any season of the year, although boots are a must in winter. The walk commences along the banks of the River Gipping as far as Sharmford Mere and Baylham Mill, and continues through the woods of Shrubland Park to Coddenham. The return is across fields and woodland. The route is well marked for most of the way.

LEAVE THE PICNIC SITE by going left on the path in front of the Information Centre; cross the road and turn left along the path bordered by a post and rail fence. In a short while cross the stile on the right and follow the path to go between two gravel pits. At this point keep straight forward towards the railway and the river. (The chimney of the cement works is straight ahead.) Turn right under the railway bridge and continue along by the river.

The lush vegetation of summer is immediately apparent with valerian, comfrey and purple loosestrife all to be seen along the bank which is covered in parts by the huge leaves of butterbur. (See Walk 3)

After crossing two stiles a lane is reached. Turn left over the bridge and, immediately after the first house, turn right into the driveway. Go 12m or so forward and look right for a narrow path beside a garage and this will lead back to the left bank of the river. (Should you miss this little alleyway you will arrive at Great Blakenham Church. If so, retrace your steps and look again!) For the next two miles the path borders the river bank, so looking for waymarks can be replaced by watching for the abundant river life.

The valley of the River Gipping was formed by the scouring action of the melting waters of glaciers at the end of the last Ice Age. The surface crag and clay was gouged down to the underlying chalk and this helps to explain the increased amount of flints in some of the nearby fields and the presence of chalk-loving plants like scabious.

In the nineteenth century the river was navigable by barges as far as Stowmarket and a large amount of agricultural produce was transported in this way into the port of Ipswich.

The river path passes by several worked-out gravel pits now the home for a wealth of fish as well as coot, heron, small flocks of Canada geese and the occasional cormorant. Keep a lookout along the river for the darting flight of a kingfisher.

Ignore the waymarked sign and the bridge over the river and continue along the bank with Sharmford Mere stretching out on the other side.

The river bank at this point is lined with Alder trees which in winter especially are very attractive with their red buds and catkins. Alders (Alnus) are interesting as the male and female parts are separate on the same tree. The male catkins are the long hanging catkins which appear in early winter and expand to produce pollen in the spring. The female are tiny erect catkins which ripen later into small woody cones. Alders are common by rivers and on marshy soils, and are easily recognised in winter by stalked side buds and in summer by the notch in the leaf at the tip of its main vein. It is a tree which used to be regularly coppiced (see Walk 18) and the hard wood was used for tool handles and the soles of clogs.

After crossing a pair of double stiles, each separated by a wooden bridge, the path soon arrives at Baylham Mill.

THE ROUTE - SOUTHERN SECTION

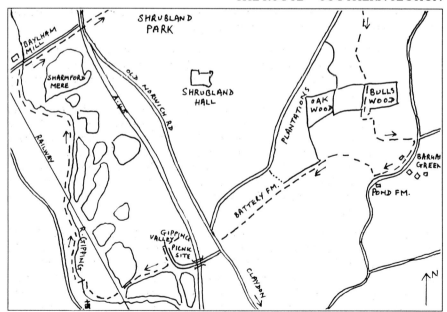

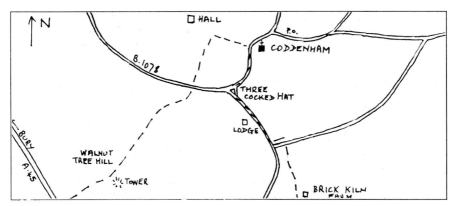

THE ROUTE - NORTHERN SECTION

A photograph of the mill in 1952 showed that, outwardly, it was in a good state of repair, but now it is showing signs of rapid deterioration. The mill itself dates from the eighteenth century although the mill house is thought to be much earlier. By the side of the mill are the lock gates, a reminder of the commercial use of the river in the past. restoration of the mill is due to start in 1994.

Turn right by the mill along a delightful narrow lane, once metalled, but now fast becoming covered with moss and creeping plants.

To the right, in the vicinity of Baylham House Farm, is the site of a Roman camp, Combretovium, which lay on the route from Camulodunum (Colchester) to Venta Icenorum (Caistor St. Edmund, just outside present-day Norwich).

Traces of foxes using the path as a thoroughfare from river to woods might be observed here. Fox droppings are sausage-shaped, about 8 - 10 cms long, and with a spirally twisted point at the end. They are usually black or grey in colour although in Autumn they may be stained red as berries are a favourite food. The fox uses its strongly scented faeces to mark its territory. Look also at the interesting diamond-shaped bark pattern on the trees lining the edge of the path just before it arrives at the road. It is the bark of the White Poplar.

Steps lead down to the A45 trunk road and, as this is a fast and busy stretch, TAKE GREAT CARE IN CROSSING TO AND FROM THE CENTRAL RESERVATION. THE TRAFFIC IS FAST SO ALLOW PLENTY OF SPACE BEFORE CROSSING. The path continues opposite, through the woods of Shrubland Hall. The track now ascends the gradual rise of Walnut Tree Hill. Ignore paths crossing at right angles, and pass the tower of Shrubland Hall. (nearly hidden by the trees in summer)

71

Baylham Mill

Shrubland Hall was originally the Suffolk home of the Earl of Sandwich who was killed at the Battle of Sole Bay off Southwold in 1672. A later owner in Victorian times, who became captivated by the architecture of Italy after a visit there, paid for it to be Italianised by Sir Charles Barry, the co-designer of the Houses of Parliament. At present the Hall is used as a health clinic.

Continue up the slope and then across open farmland, past two farm cottages and an attractive house to reach the B1078 road.
If you do not wish to make the short detour to visit the village of Coddenham, turn right at the road and bear right at the next junction marked on the map as the Three Cocked Hat.
To visit Coddenham, cross straight over the B1078 to the stile. The path to the village crosses a meadow to a plank bridge. Go forward and at the next stile turn right onto a track which leads to the road opposite the church.

Coddenham Church has a fine double-hammerbeam roof, and its calm peaceful atmosphere is perhaps one reason for the long reign of many of its Vicars during the last two centuries. There are many attractive houses in the village street amongst which is the fifteenth century timber-framed house once an inn and now the Post Office.

From the church go left to the Three Cocked Hat junction (see above) and there bear left. In about half a mile, past the Italianate lodge to Shrubland Hall, turn left down a lane, and in 50m take the footpath on the right through the wood. Cross the first plank bridge and bear right along by the hedge to the next bridge. Here turn right over a third bridge and then immediately left to head towards Brick Kiln Farm. Go past the farm and continue over the next field (signed past the farm pond) keeping the hedge on your left. Then head diagonally across the second field towards the thatched cottage and the gateway in the corner of Bull's Wood. Keep on through the wood and follow its edge to the end to reach a field.

In the winter, Dog's Mercury (see Walk 16) grows at the edge of the wood.

Here turn left and in 12m turn right across the field towards a tiny thatched cottage. (The path across may have been ploughed up!) Here, if the field has been ploughed, the surface is littered with flints denoting the closeness of the underlying chalk.

Follow the track on the left of the cottage to Barham Green and then turn right to go past the houses as far as Pond Farm which, as its name suggests, has a large pond at the side. Almost opposite the pond a path leads off to the right and follows a hedge on the left as far as a plank bridge over a ditch. Cross and continue to the right along the hedge for some way to eventually overlook Broomwalk Covert and then to enter the plantation. Emerging from the woods the path goes downhill, past hen houses to return to the Norwich road and the picnic site.

73

WALK 11: CELEBRATING THE DEBEN
Kirton, Hemley and Newbourne

Start: *Kirton, Lodge Farm. Grid Ref: 283409*
O.S.Map: *Landranger 169 Pathfinder 1031*
Distance: *4 ½ miles*
Time: *2 ½ hours*
Parking: *At the head of the concrete farm road reached from Park Lane, Kirton.*
Refreshments: *The Fox, Newbourne.*

A gentle walk to Hemley by way of Kirton Creek and a short stretch of marsh, then across farmland to Newbourne with the chance of a welcome half-way pint at the Newbourne Fox. The route then continues through Newbourne and across fields back to the start point.

IGNORE THE CONCRETE ROAD leading to the buildings of Kirton Lodge Farm and walk towards the cottage which is visible further down the lane. At the cottage bear right and, in a short while, go between the buildings of Sluice Farm and across a small field towards a pair of farm gates. Cross the fence by the right hand gate to join a sandy track which slopes down towards the river. At the top of the rise turn left and drop down to Kirton Creek. (See Walk 1) After mounting the river wall continue in the same direction to go round the creek.
Where the wall ends by the copse bear right to follow the path which is raised just above the level of the marsh.

The tiny village of Hemley is soon in view and the path passes an old mooring channel for barges. The stone for building Hemley Church was landed here and in earlier times salt was manufactured at Hemley and shipped to Woodbridge.

After passing the channel the route then veers left away from the river, passing a small pond to join a lane near a cottage. Continue forward past the church, and where the road bends right, follow the track straight ahead between a cottage and a bungalow.
After crossing a field the track edges along the left of Ranglins Wood to descend into an interesting area named on the map as Puddingpokes. Cross the meadow keeping the trees and a young plantation on the right. Go through a pair of farm gates and continue in the same direction to pass a stand of tall trees. Then veer left to follow a somewhat indistinct path, and a stile will be observed ahead at the bottom of the shallow valley.
Cross the edge along by the stream and then continue diagonally across a marshy, reed-covered patch aiming for the tower of Newbourne Church which is now

visible. The path across may be indistinct and boggy but in winter the rotting reeds act as a raft. Head for the tall tree and the path then becomes more obvious on the right of the hedge to lead across the recreation field to the Village Hall.

Here, if you would welcome a drink and a rest, turn right and continue right at the junction to arrive at the Fox.

Newbourne Church has several points of interest amongst which is the scratching of a mediaeval, three-masted ship on the west jamb of the porch.

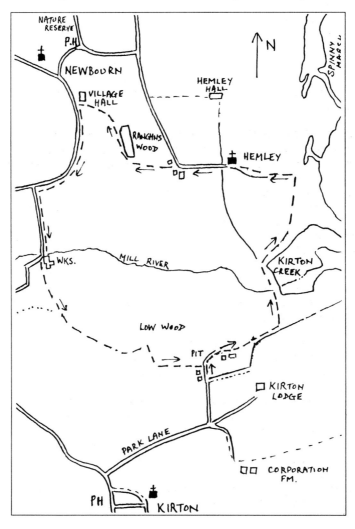

The ship is of a type common in the late fifteenth century and was possibly done by a Newbourne sailor who worked from the then busy port of Goseford. The font is carved with lions and 'wild men of the woods'. In the great storm of 1987 the east window and wall of the church was blown out, but a new one was dedicated two years later. This includes the face of Christ which survived intact amongst the shattered glass of the old window. In the churchyard there is a sad inscription on the tombstone of the Suffolk giant, one George Page, who reputedly stood seven feet, seven inches tall.

Retrace your steps past the Village Hall and continue for just over half a mile past the greenhouses which used to be part of the Land Settlement Association.

The cottages were originally set up as part of government policy to aid unemployed miners at the end of World War 1. Each 'settler' became a member of a Land Settlement Association and was given five acres of land and a new house with piggeries, outbuildings and a greenhouse. Practical advice was given as well as aid with tools. The Association was wound up in the late 1980's and since then most of the original cottages have been enlarged. However, many greenhouses remain in production.

Bear left at the junction and proceed to a humped bridge at the side of the Anglian Water Authority pumping station. Just past this, leave the road by mounting the bank on the bend of the road and take the marked path that leads to open fields. The path 'wiggles' slightly left to continue on the left of the tall hedge eventually crossing a stream by a small plank bridge.
Cross over the meadow to the stile and follow the path behind a cottage to join a farm track. Here turn left, and after a short rise past the copse, continue forward keeping the hedge on the right.

There is now a good view of the River Deben and, if the right spot is chosen, on a clear day it is possible to see the towers of five churches.

The track then dips down to a small stream. Follow the bend left and continue up the slope to the hedge at the top. Follow the path left between the hedges and at the track turn right, back to the start point.

WALK 12: WALL AND MOAT
Parham to Easton

Start: *Parham. Grid Ref: 307607*

O.S.Map: *Landranger 156 .*

Distance: *5½ miles*

Time: *2½ hours*

Parking: *Parham is on the B1116 to Framlingham, north of Wickham Market. Turn right over the bridge in the middle of the village to park near the telephone box.*

Refreshments: *The White Horse, Easton.*

A pleasant walk across fields and through woods to the attractive village of Easton. At some points the route, for the early part of the walk, is not always clear but the return by lane and field to Parham is easy. The walk concludes by passing close to Moat Hall, an Elizabethan moated manor house.

FROM THE TELEPHONE BOX go straight across the B1116 to the signpost marking a path up the bank. Go round the farm buildings and bear left diagonally over a small field to the hedge where there is a felled tree trunk. Keep the farm buildings immediately behind and go away from the farm along a short length of hedge. Then follow the shallow ditch which heads at right angles away from the road across arable land.

To the right, after passing a lone ash tree, the tower of Framlingham Church and the battlements of the castle can be seen on the skyline.

Where the ditch ends, continue forward as far as the three-branched signpost. Here bear right and in a few metres turn left and head towards the electricity pylon along a well-marked track which runs by the side of the wood.

In late summer the wood is edged by rose bay willow herb.

Cross the open space and pass under the electricity power line to enter the wood, Sally's Grove, by the signpost. In a few metres, where the track forks, bear left keeping the new plantation on the right.

Here, even in summer, the track is very wet and boggy with some interesting flowers and sedges.

Continue through the wood and bear left at the next signpost. In 40m turn right and then almost immediately left to follow the field edge round the right side of Maid's Wood to a yellow marker which can be seen ahead at the edge of the trees. Pass the marker and continue forward to the next corner. Cross the plank bridge over the ditch and go on as far as the boundary wall of the by-gone Easton Park. (The wall is somewhat hidden by the hedge). Ignore the sign to the right and go on in the same direction with the trees now on the right.

77

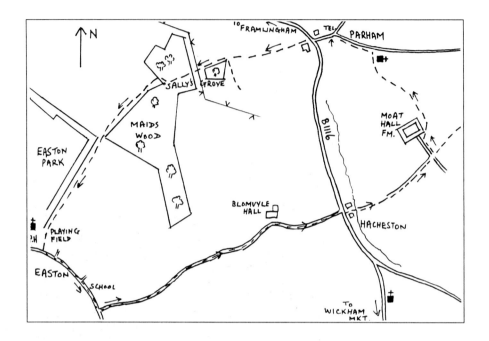

In a short while there is a good view south towards Wickham Market Church, one of the few churches in Suffolk with a spire. Perhaps spires were not generally thought feasible in the area because of the strong easterly winds. In the past the spire was visible at sea and was used as a landmark for shipping along the coast.

On the right, between gaps in the undergrowth, is evidence of the crinkle-crankle wall which surrounded Easton Park but which is now sadly in a state of decay.

The path skirts the village cricket ground, the bowling green and the graveyard (what a lovely combination!) to descend into the village. Notice the osier beds behind the cottages opposite the end of the track. A short detour right may now be made to the White Horse for refreshment.

The church and a well-preserved stretch of the crinkle-crankle wall are nearby. Easton Park house has been pulled down although some of the original outbuildings can still be seen through the imposing gateway.

Retrace your steps back along the street and up the hill past the village school as far as the turn signposted to Hacheston. The route now continues along this lane as far as Hacheston village.

Moat Hall, Parham

Almost immediately opposite the junction with the village street is an opening by the side of a small builder's yard. Take this, going between hedges and over a small bridge crossing a stream. Follow the path up the hill to the farm and here turn left towards Moat Hall. Cross a stile on the right in front of the imposing gateway, and head round the side of the house and moat.

The Hall was built early in the sixteenth century. It is a timber-framed house, but on the north and west side there is a lot of attractive herring-bone brickwork and some tall windows. The imposing gateway has carvings of Wild Men. Pevsner rates it as one of the most picturesque moated halls in Suffolk.

The path mounts the mound at the side of the moat and then descends across fields by way of three gates to the side of Parham Church.

On the way back to the start point look out for the oriel window of Church Farm house and its sill carved with animals, shield and a human figure.

WALK 13: BURIALS AND COMMONS
Sutton Hoo to Methersgate

Start: *Alderton and Hollesley Road Junction on B1083, one mile from Melton. Grid Ref: 297492,*

O.S.Map: *Landranger 169. Pathfinder 1031*

Distance: *7 miles*

Time: *4 hours*

Parking: *On waste ground adjacent to golf course and near junction.*

Refreshments: *The halfway point at 'The Hams' is a good spot for a picnic.*

This can be a bracing walk if the wind is blowing by the river or across the open common on the return half. The walk takes in the Sutton Hoo burial site of which there are brief details on Page 83. There are good views of Woodbridge from across the river and the route crosses Sutton Common to meet the river further downstream.

LEAVE ON THE FOOTPATH opposite the parking area across the B1083 (signposted 'to Sutton Hoo Burial site'). Follow this path to the end of the spruce grove and keep straight on to the site. After visiting the burial site (if open, see notes) descend the slope past the site entrance and at the bottom bear right to go past a large house. Turn left between house and barn and on reaching the open field keep left along by the edge of a wood. Cross a bridge to the river wall. Go left soon to edge away from the river up a rise between tall sycamore trees. The path then drops back to the river's edge to afford excellent views across to Woodbridge with its quays and the church on Market Hill.
Ignore the first set of steps up the slope to the left and continue along past a 'boggy bit' until reaching a small ruined hut.

Almost opposite now is a good view of Woodbridge Tidemill with its mansard roof and dormer windows. A tidemill has been in this place since 1170, although the present one dates from the seventeenth century. It is believed to be the last working tidemill in Great Britain, ceasing operation in 1956 when the oak shaft of the water wheel broke. The mill then fell into disrepair but has since been restored to working condition and is open to visitors.

The path now turns left and bends back on itself up the slope of the cliff. Turn right by a copse of pines soon to bear left up a gradual slope. Go right at the top along the edge of a second copse.

Across the river it is possible to pick out the entrance to Martlesham Creek with Kyson Point guarding the inlet.

Do not follow the copse round to the left but veer slightly left diagonally across the field (which may be cultivated) to the signpost which is somewhat hidden in the hedge. Cross the lane and go forward, over a second lane, towards Methersgate Hall which can be seen ahead at the end of the next field. Pass through the metal farm gate and carry on to the Hall.

> To the right there is an open view across the river to British Telecom's Research Station built in 1972. At the beginning of this century much of the land either side of the River Deben was open and treeless like this space and it was not until the 1920s that considerable tree planting took place.

Veer right at the lane and go between the barns and down the track by the side of the Hall. Turn left a little further on by a brick wall up a short grassy slope and then over two stiles. In 100m turn right. This is 'Point A' to which the route returns later. Go down towards the river by crossing three stiles and a paddock in succession. After the third stile go to the corner of the field diagonally opposite and through the fence to arrive at Methersgate Quay.

> Here until 1918 there was a small warehouse and river trade with local farms. Earlier in the Middle Ages, Methersgate was a landing place for the Manor of Campsey in Sutton, but the name Methersgate did not originate until the seventeenth century when a Robert Mather lived nearby. The suffix 'gate' was an early name for the 'hard' or stone causeway which gave access over the mud to ferries and barges. In the time of Queen Elizabeth I, larger farms were obliged by law to grow a crop of flax or hemp and a storage house for the local crop existed at Methersgate Quay.

A pleasant place for a halfway rest and maybe a sandwich exists further along the shore at a point on the map known as The Hams. Turn left down river and depending on the state of the tide, edge along the foreshore or the neighbouring field to The Hams, a wooded area edged by a stretch of beach and a low sandy cliff.

> Fallen trees provide plenty of places to sit and to observe feeding wildfowl and waders. At my last visit there were large flocks of shelduck and oystercatchers.

The route now returns to 'Point A' (see above)

At this point do not return to the Hall with its cannons on the lawn, but go forward with backs to the river straight across the field to a lane. Cross the lane to the stile opposite and follow the fence to the fallen tree where you cross the stile and stream on the left. Follow the path over the 'boggy and nettly bit' to a sandy farm track. (If 'the bit' proves to be impassable for any reason it may be necessary to return to the lane and go on to the farm a short way ahead and find the sandy track going right from there.)

At the track turn right, bearing left after the barn, marked on the map as Newshill

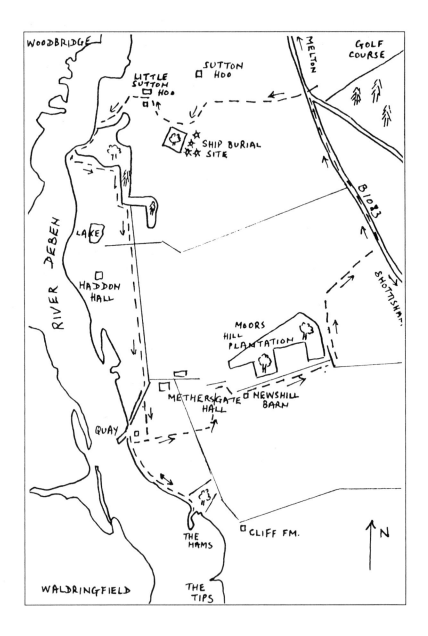

Barn, (what famous news was brought there I wonder?) and continue for some way until reaching the end of a copse and a crossing of tracks.
Turn left at the 'crossroads' and in a short while bear left again to go alongside a patch of gorse, birch scrub and a few trees. Is this area a remnant of what Sutton Heath used to be like? At the next crossing of tracks, by a hawthorn and a few pines, turn right and head across the open field to the road which can be observed ahead. At the road turn left and return in about half a mile to the start point.

Sutton Hoo Burial Site.

The first recorded dig at the site was in 1863 although the burial mounds had been robbed as early as the seventeenth century. The discovery of the Anglo-Saxon ship burial was made by Basil Brown in 1939 when, with the help of experts from the then Ministry of Works and Edinburgh University, the impression of a ship nearly 30 metres long was uncovered together with an adjacent chamber containing the possessions of a dead man. These included a large silver dish, a superb helmet, gold and silver jewellery, precious sword buckles and a sceptre which indicated a royal burial thought now to be that of Raedwald, an East Anglian king, 599 - 624.

Since then there have been other excavations notably 1965 - 70 and more recently from 1984 onwards when trenches were dug and artifacts such as pottery and flints were discovered indicating the continuous use of the site since Neolithic and Bronze Age times. 'Sand bodies' were discovered - the outlines of bodies etched in the sand - and attempts were made, using modern polymers, to preserve them. Carbon dating of one of these yielded a date of c.700 AD suggesting that the area had been used as a buriel site for at least most of the seventh century.

At the moment of writing the future possibility of visits to the site remain doubtful. At the end of the 1993 season it was agreed that no further excavations would take place to avoid damage to any graves that remained. The site was restored and closed.

As one walks down to the river, however, it is easy to appreciate the difficulties involved in dragging the thirty metre long buriel ship up from the river to the site where it was discovered.

Further details of the excavations and discoveries can be found at the museum on Market Hill in Woodbridge.

WALK 14: RIVER AND RESERVOIR
Stutton and Tattingstone

Start: *Stutton. Grid Ref: 142347*
O.S.Map: *Landranger 169*
Distance: *4 miles*
Time: *2 hours*
Parking: *Stutton Community Hall. (Space designated for walkers)*
Refreshments: *The Kings Head, Stutton*

This is an easy walk which takes you first across farmland, along the River Stour at its widest point and then returning by a quiet track to Stutton. On a sunlit day the stretch along the river is not to be missed. There is a seaside feel to the area with extensive views and some woodland and it is an important site for wildlife.

From the Community Hall walk towards the village centre and in about 80m take the footpath on the right marked by the white gate which leads to Crepping Hall.

The track here is lined on the left by a row of holly bushes and on the right by tall Black Poplar trees. This variety of poplar has glossy green buds in early autumn which later turn dark brown. The bark of the tree is deeply fissured vertically.

Ignore the path which soon crosses at right angles and continue forward past the Hall at which point the track becomes a path across fields.

Veer left to meet the river bank further on and then continue right either along the beach or alongside the field edge at the top of the cliff to arrive at Stutton Ness.

With Holbrook Bay to the left, the Stour reaches its widest point and especially at low tide the area is thronged with birds. In the winter months it is a favourite feeding area for Brent geese which together with shelduck are usually the largest birds to be seen here. The Brent can easily be distinguished from the Canada goose by its smaller size and the absence of the white patch on the cheek. The adult brents do, however, have a white mark on the neck and all have an obvious white undertail. They divide into two races, the pale-bellied and the dark-bellied, but generally they have a burned or smokey appearance. They graze on salt flats and river-side fields often in large flocks but towards the end of the winter they are beginning to separate into smaller groups and pairs. Flight is swift in irregular flocks as they are small enough not to fly in a 'V' formation. When sitting on water they can sometimes be confused with ducks with their similar tail-up profile.

Continue up-river

Along the edge of the cliff top are large patches of Alexanders, a member of the parsley family, easily recognisable from their umbrella-like heads. The unusual name derives from the fact that the plant is a herb of Macedonia, Alexander the Great's kingdom. Its black seeds, which are favourites for finches in the autumn, had a variety of uses by herbalists including the cure of flatulence and snakebite. The plant is edible; leaves as a herb, stalks like asparagus and even the roots can be a substitute for parsnips. Its yellow flowers appear in April.

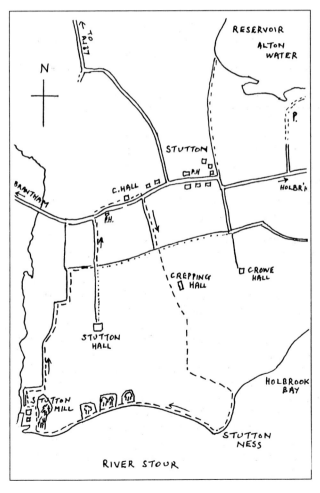

Another plant growing nearby is Weld, a member of the Mignonette family, with its tall spikes of yellowish green flowers. Later the spikes are lined with globular seed pods open at the top and divided into three lobes. In medieval times weld was used by dyers to colour cloth yellow. It is a heliotropic plant - one which turns its flowers towards the sun.

Further along, the cliff edge is lined by blackthorn heavy with sloe berries in September. Look out, too, for the Spindle-tree shrub with its seeds contained in a four-lobed fruit which glows pink in the autumn.

The path enters the first of three patches of mixed woodland consisting mainly of oak, sweet chestnut and larch. Ignore worn paths leading off to the right and continue forward. After the third wood which is entered by crossing a small wooden bridge go over a shallow ditch and pass round the edge of the field to Stutton Mill.

Turn right before reaching the house to go between the paddock fence and hedge up the slope, through a gap in the hedge at the top, and then left round the field by the side of the buildings to reach the track which gradually mounts the slope of the valley to pass a farm cottage and the remains of other farm buildings on the left. Further on, after passing a red-brick cottage, turn right along the side of the wood, and where the track crosses the drive, go left towards the lodge house and the road.

In the opposite direction is a fine vista towards Stutton Hall, one of several halls built on the ridge to enjoy the view over the Stour valley. Both Stutton Hall and Crepping Hall are on the sites of old manors mentioned in Domesday.

A little way along, the drive passes between two oak trees which are interesting to compare. The one on the left is a Turkey Oak which has a different leaf shape to the more common oak on the right. Check whether the latter is the English oak or a Sessile. The English or Pedunculate oak has its acorns on long stalks or peduncles, while on the Sessile they are in groups.

At the road turn right to return to the start point.

WALK 15: CELEBRATING SUFFOLK CHURCHES
Blythburgh to Wenhaston

Start: *Blythburgh Church. Grid Ref: 451754*
O.S.Map: *Landranger 156.*
Distance: *5 miles*
Time: *3 hours*
Parking: *Car park adjoining church.*
Refreshments: *The Star Inn, Wenhaston.*

> *An easy walk along the bank of the River Blyth to the village of Wenhaston with its interesting church. A detour to the south-west of the village and the hamlet of Blackheath may be made before returning to Blythburgh Church, the 'cathedral of the marshes'.*

From the car park return to the lane in front of the church turning left to follow the lane round to meet the A12. Continue left along the A12 as far as the bridge over the River Blyth and take the footpath which goes left along the river bank on the far side of the bridge.

> At a point opposite the church is the site of the Priory which was founded in the twelfth century by King Henry I and which was suppressed by Cardinal Wolsey in 1528.

The path runs along the reed-edged bank for some way until it reaches two barbed wire fences separated by 10m. Cross these and go left along the line of the fence. On the right the ground rises to a patch of heathland and exposed gravel. In a short while re-cross a similar double fence to continue along the bank of the river between the reeds.

> The river, aided by the encroachment of the reeds, has now narrowed. In the fifteenth century the Blyth carried a prosperous trade in fish, corn and wool, and the magnificent church at Blythburgh was built with the wealth that resulted from this trade. Even as early as 1066 Blythburgh must have been of considerable importance since the town then was the hereditary possession of the King. Its glebe, detailed in Domesday Book, was ten times the average size for the country. However, the increasing use of larger ships with deeper draughts and the growth of the coastal spit near Southwold diverted future trade to Dunwich and other nearby ports. The town began to decline, and apart from being the site of a military barracks in Georgian times and later a stage on the old railway to Southwold, it never recovered its prosperity.

Ignore the first crossing point over the river and cross at the second bridge, which

is just past Blythburgh Hospital, the large building on the ridge to the right.

> The Hospital is the successor of the old Poor House for the area which in 1878 housed as many as 558 paupers.

The path goes straight forward from the bridge across Blower's Common with two double stiles to cross. Fifty metres after a sharp turn to the left, a stile leads to a farm track. Walk past the farmhouse and continue along the track bearing right at a junction of footpaths to arrive on the outskirts of Wenhaston indicated by a row of bungalows on the left. Go forward along the lane to arrive at the cross-roads by the village Hall and the church.

> St. Peter's Church was originally under the patronage of Blythburgh Priory, but like many Suffolk churches was founded on the site of a Saxon church. It suffered extensive damage at the hands of William Dowsing's men in Cromwellian times and the 'Doom' or Last Judgement painting, believed to be by a monk from the Priory, survived because it had been whitewashed to comply with a Parliamentary order passed earlier in 1545. The painting originally hung in the chancel arch and during restoration work in 1892 it was taken down and placed in the churchyard. Heavy rain washed away the whitewash to reveal the painting which had been hidden from view for over three hundred years. Pevsner, in the Suffolk edition of

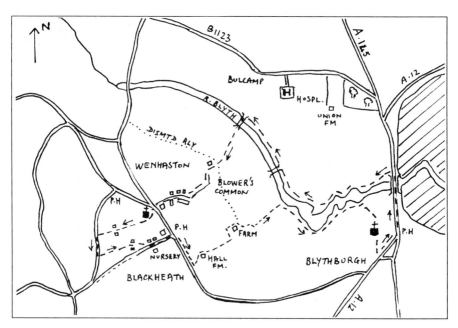

his 'Buildings of England' describes the painting as 'distressingly rustic' but Cautley in his book on Suffolk Churches thinks it is delightful. Whom do you agree with? (A detailed description of the painting is provided by the church).

On leaving the churchyard, turn right down the lane which soon develops on to a way-marked path heading straight across a field towards a small farm. Go past the farm to join a metalled lane and here turn left. In a short while turn left again opposite a footpath sign on the right and follow the track up the slope, keeping left to pass some cottages on Wenhaston Black Heath, a hummocky and gorse-covered remnant of the old heathland. Look for the yellow fire hydrant adjacent to a pink-washed cottage, and soon after this bear right past a small pond down a narrow gorse-lined path. After wending between houses the path reaches Hog Lane. Here turn left past a small garden nursery to join the Blythburgh road. The Star Inn is to the left of the junction.

The walk continues to the right and, in about a quarter of a mile, turn left onto a footpath about 100m past the entrance to Hall Farm. Go diagonally across the field to a stile on the left of the farm buildings and then, with the barns on the right, go forward to the field behind. The path follows the hedge on the right across two fields. At the end of the second field follow the fence left in order to go through a second farmyard. Passing between the farm buildings, bear right on the track (note the disused railway on the left), cross a bridge over a gully and in 100m go left to a stile. Cross this and another stile will be seen a short way on the left. From here move to the right of the gully opposite and head forward to the southern bank of the River Blyth. This leads without further difficulty back to Blythburgh Church.

A licence to build Holy Trinity Church was granted to the Priory in 1412 and, for a town large enough to have its own mint and gaol and the grant of two annual fairs, a small church would obviously not 'do'. The resulting building illustrates the golden age of the Perpendicular style and its roof must be one of the best in the country.

After various vicissitudes, including a fire in 1438, the collapse of the steeple in the great storm of 1577, the destruction wrought by Dowsing in 1644 and the neglect suffered in the nineteenth century, restoration of the building we see today began in 1881 and still goes on.

There is much of interest in the church; the pairs of angels supporting the roof; the lively carvings on the bench ends depicting the seven deadly sins and the four seasons; the choir stalls with the carvings of the Apostles and Saints, each carrying their own emblems; and the schoolboy carving on the book-rest of Dirck Lowersen 1665 - was he the son of a Dutchman brought over to advise on land drainage? But do not miss the narrow, circular stone staircase in the angle of the south and west walls which leads up to the Priest's Room with its quiet meditative atmosphere.

WALK 16: IN THE STEPS OF THE WOOL TRADE
Hadleigh to Kersey

Start: *Hadleigh Grid Ref: 025422*
O.S.Map: *Landranger 155*
Distance: *5 miles*
Time: *2 hours*
Parking: *Adjoining Hadleigh Riverside Walks picnic area down Duke Street (a turning on the right to Lower Layham) south of Hadleigh Church.*
Refreshments: *Pubs and teashops in Hadleigh or Kersey.*

Starting by the side of the River Brett in Hadleigh a well-marked route leads across fields to one of the most picturesque villages in Suffolk. With the church prominent on the hill-top, Kersey's old houses straggle up the slopes of a valley on either side of a ford which crosses the main street. The return to Hadleigh concludes with a walk through a small nature reserve beside the River Brett.

Hadleigh is a small market town situated midway between Ipswich and Sudbury in countryside noticeably more rolling than in the east of the county. A stroll along its main street and the close around the church and guildhall may well prove interesting. Hadleigh's charter as a market town dates from 1252, and by 1568 only Ipswich and Bury were more wealthy than Hadleigh - wealth which had accumulated from being the centre of the cloth making industry. The church and many of the town houses are witness to the success of the trade which lasted until the woollen industry moved north to Yorkshire in the seventeenth century. However, James John Hissey writing later said "I know not of a more attractive town possessing as it does a delightful air of mellowness and old time calm so grateful and rare in this busy money making age" - a comment which still rings true today.

LEAVE THE PARKING SPOT keeping the picnic area fence on the right and follow the path which runs parallel to the river but outside the riverside reserve. (The church spire is soon visible ahead through the trees.) Bear left up the slope of the field with the blackthorn hedge on your right. Pass the entrance to Broom Hill Reserve and continue up with the hedge now on the left.
Leaving the wood on the right go past a wartime pillbox to the top of the knoll and then left to the crest of the hill marked by a stunted oak tree.
Continue along the path keeping the hedge on the right until arriving at a track marked by a signpost and here turn right towards a farm.

In spring time the bank by the side of the track is thick with Dog's Mercury and there are clumps of primroses and wild arum with its spear-shaped leaves. Dog's Mercury blooms from February to April and has small greenish flowers. It is highly poisonous and has a pungent smell attracting midges which in turn help to pollinate the flowers. The plant gets its name from the fact that in earlier times it was considered fit only for dogs. It was described by Nicholas Culpeper, the seventeenth century herbalist, as being the most fatal plant in the country.

The walk towards the farm allows extensive views over the surrounding Suffolk countryside and the villages of Elmsett and Whatfield. Turn left at the road and continue to the A1071 passing Coram Farm on the left. At the junction by the pond turn left, and in about 50m take the footpath on the right marked 'Kersey Vale'. The path drops down to the vale crossing a small stream by a wooden bridge and then turns right along a tarmac track. Ignore a footpath to the right and continue up the slope to arrive at the southern end of the village and St.Mary's Church.

Although the southern wall of the church dates from the twelfth century, the church was greatly enlarged in the fourteenth century and the tower was finally completed about 1481 after a long delay caused by the Black Death a hundred years earlier.

Like many churches in the area the building suffered during the Reformation when the rood screen was destroyed and the walls whitewashed. Six panels from the screen, decorated with pictures of prophets and kings, were discovered in a local farm and these now stand in the north aisle.

If time allows, a stroll down the street from the church may be made to view the interesting and attractive houses of which Woodbine Cottage, first built early in the fifteenth century, is probably the oldest. River House has an Elizabethan brick porch, while the houses opposite the Post Office and the White Horse Inn further up the hill are also worth seeing.

Then return to the church and on leaving the churchyard turn left along the road signposted Hadleigh/Bildeston. A little further on take the first footpath on the right across the field to the hedge, turning left to follow it round the edge of the field. Cross the short open space, head towards the house and then continue to follow another hedge to a farm track. Here turn left and in 100m turn right aiming towards the main road visible on the ridge opposite.

Cross a bridge over a stream before the rise. The path is not so obvious here but head for a small oak tree with a sapling beside it. Go round the oak and then follow the bank as it winds towards the road. The path drops down through a gap in the blackthorn hedge and then continues to the wooden farm gates at the roadside.

On the slope up to the road there are several patches of Colt's-foot growing, one of the first wildflowers to bloom between February and April. It flowers before the leaves appear, giving rise to its other name 'son before father'. The hoof shaped leaves - hence Colt's Foot - were used in the past to treat asthma, and liquid from them helped make a linctus for coughs. Its Linnaean name, Tussilago, comes from the Greek 'tussis' meaning cough. You will notice that it differs from the Dandelion in having a central disc as well as ray florets.

Cross the road to the gate opposite and go diagonally left across a short stretch of field to a narrow path between hedges. On arriving at a small estate road turn right and go straight forward as far as the cemetery which the path avoids by going across the neighbouring sports field to a track by the side of the River Brett. Turn right at the track and then pass through the gate on the left into the reserve continuing along the path for about half a mile back to the parking spot.

The reserve is a delight at any time of the year. In spring clumps of Marsh Marigold are already sending up their brilliant yellow flowers to brighten the more sombre trees and you may notice here and there carpets of Moschatel, a tiny plant with greenish flowers. Examine it closely and you will see that the flowerhead is actually five flowers - four facing outwards and one upwards - from which its other name 'town-hall clock' arises. It is the only one of its species and is common in woods.

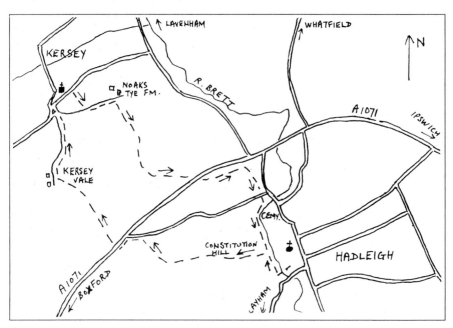

WALK 17: TINKER'S MARSHES
Walberswick

Start: *Walberswick. Grid Ref: 484745*
O.S.Map: *Landranger 156*
Distance: *5 miles*
Time: *2 ½ hours*
Parking: *Hoist Covert Car Park. (On entering Walberswick turn right after passing the church and double back down the by road for about half a mile).*
Refreshments: *The Bell or The Anchor*

> *After crossing part of what, in earlier centuries, was a sheep walk, the route then traverses a Nature Conservancy reserve which is rich in bird life - an added interest to a very beautiful stretch of unspoilt river. A visit to Southwold or a more leisurely exploration of Walberswick itself may be made before returning to the start point.*

THERE ARE TWO PATHS that leave from Hoist Covert. For this walk leave the car park by a gap in the fence opposite the information board and cross the neighbouring field to the main Walberswick road. Here turn left away from the village and in about 100m take the path on the right that goes diagonally across the heath back towards Walberswick.

> This heathland, known as Tinker's Walk, was part of an extensive area used for sheep farming. Domesday Book recorded flocks of sheep in the area, but the industry reached its height in the seventeenth and eighteenth centuries. Arthur Young, a writer on agriculture, visiting the area in 1795, noted a flock of one thousand, six hundred on one farm. He wrote, 'dry heaths are to be profitably managed only by sheep being made the principal object'. The sheep walks were carefully managed by being cut and burnt to produce a good crop of ling. The heather and gorse were also used for bedding and ditch repair work. The decline began at the end of the nineteenth century with the change in farming methods but it is interesting that in the 1990s, with the cut-backs in cereal growing, flocks of sheep seem once again a familiar sight.

Cross the first track and continue forward until arriving at a gate and fence. Bear left, keeping the fence on the right, and walk towards the lone house, Tinker's Barn. The path cuts left in front of the house and after crossing a stile between some trees go straight forward over a field to a track which crosses at right angles. Turn right down the track towards the second cottage, Tinker's House.

> A little way along the track is a short length of blackthorn hedge. If it is

March or April look out for Spring Beauty which covers the ground under the hedge and adds its delicate white flowers to the creamy white of the blackthorn. Spring Beauty may have come to this country from America where another name for it is Indian Lettice, since the leaves were valued by the Indians as a source of food. The flower appears to come from the centre of the leaf caused by the fact that the upper leaves are joined in pairs and this makes the plant easily recognisable.

The path carries on to the left of the house across a scrubby patch of land to the river bank and continues to the right. From now on the walk follows the river for nearly two miles, so relax and enjoy the scenery!

The land on the right of the river, Tinker's Marshes, is cut by several drainage channels, and there are a number of pools and meres which support a varied bird life apart from the gullies of the river itself. Shelduck, oystercatchers, dunlin and even some avocet are all to be seen here, and you may be lucky like we were to see a hen harrier hunting low over the marshes.

Further on the bank forks into two. Be careful to take the inner bank as there is a break in the one nearest the river. After passing the ruins of an old windmill on the far side, a footbridge over the river is reached.

Over the years there have been three types of ferry at this point prior to the

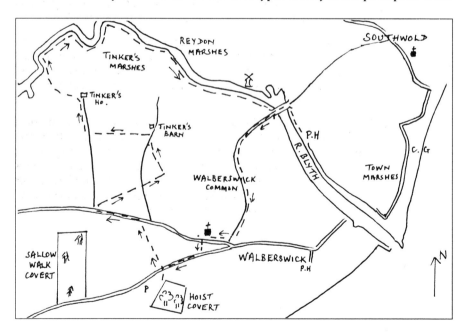

94

bridge being built, rowing boat, chain ferry and steamboat.

The distance so far walked is three miles. If you have the time and energy you may wish to extend the walk into Southwold by crossing the bridge and bearing right along the far bank to meet a footpath which crosses Town Marshes and arrives in the town south of the church. The return route to the bridge can be varied by walking down the coast, past the coastguard lookout to the river estuary, and then back along the footpath on the north bank of the River Blyth - an additional three miles from leaving the bridge.

The return to Walberswick is along the metalled lane that leads from the bridge. This soon becomes gorse-lined and eventually arrives in the village. Turn right at the road (unless you wish to explore the village) and about 50m past the church take a cut on the left that leads between the houses to return to the road. Here bear right for the short walk back to Hoist Covert.

The ninety foot high tower of the church of St. Andrews was commenced in 1426, the masons being Richard Russel of Dunwich and Adam Powle of Blythburgh. The design copied those of Tunstall and Halesworth and was built with walls six feet thick. Work was to be done in the summer only (for obvious reasons! - but see Page 18) and materials and a house to live in were provided. Their pay was '40 scheelyngs of laughful money of Inglond; and a cade of full Herynge eche year, in tyme of werkyng; and eche of hem a Gowne of lenore, ones in the tyme of werkyng.'

Although the church suffered during the Protectorate, a beautiful medieval pulpit survived - perhaps because of the Puritan love of sermons! - and a rare alter stone has been set in the alter. The alter cross and candlesticks are unusual being made by members of the congregation out of driftwood found on the beach.

At the end of the nineteenth century Walberswick was a centre for artists attracted by the clear light and the seashore. The most famous of the group was perhaps Philip Wilson Steer (1860 - 1942) an impressionist painter, many of whose paintings featured the dazzling light of the nearby seashore and the children playing on the beach. The daughter of a local fisherman was a model for some of his pictures. His work reflects the carefree days of summers past and Walberswick today still presents a leisurely, tranquil air.

WALK 18: A WALK THRU' TWO WOODLANDS
Bentley

Start: *Bentley, near Capel St. Mary, Ipswich. Grid Ref: 110368*
O.S.Map: *Landranger 169. Pathfinder 1053.*
Distance: *4 miles*
Time: *2 hours*
Parking: *Village Hall Car Park, Bentley.*
Refreshments: *The Case is Altered, Bentley. The Royal Oak, East End.*

> *Although this walk may be enjoyed at any time of the year, a good time is in the Spring when the bluebells are out and before the trees are fully in leaf. This makes it easier to identify birds such as warblers and other summer visitors. The route goes through two woods which are full of interest to the naturalist and to those interested in woodland management.*

ON LEAVING THE CAR PARK turn left and walk past The Case is Altered. In a short while take the footpath on the left which cuts diagonally across the field opposite a house called Wayside. Aim for a horse chestnut tree near the right hand edge of the wood. Here a short slope drops down by the side of a small young plantation to meet the path through the wood. Turn left and in a few metres bear right to follow the path which runs parallel to the stream at the edge of the wood.

> In springtime swathes of bluebells and wood anemones stretch between the trees, the latter favouring the edge of the wood as they need more light. Wood anemones, or windflowers as they are sometimes called, grow well in deciduous woods, but the flowers close in cloudy weather or at the end of the day. The white flower has an unpleasant smell and the juice of the plant is both bitter and poisonous. Neither the anemone or the bluebell survive long if picked. (Collecting flowers or plants from the woods is, in any case, forbidden)
> Bluebells depend on their leaves for food and the plant dies if these are crushed under foot. In Elizabethan times, they were known as 'crowtoes' and starch from the bulbs was used to stiffen the ornate ruffs worn by the gentry.
> Clumps of marsh marigold grow by the stream and wild lily of the valley grow by the path.

Ignore the path which soon branches left up the slope between pine trees and continue in the same direction up the rise past some birch trees and then, in a short while, bear right along a mossy path bordered on the right by young birch but on the left by coppiced sweet chestnut trees.

The Sweet or Spanish Chestnut (Castanea) was introduced into this country by the Romans in order to raise their nuts which were a staple food for their legionaries. The tree is easily recognised by its large long-oval leaf which has distinct veins each ending in a sharp tooth. It is a very vigorous tree and if left to grow will rapidly increase to a girth of eight or nine metres. They are also long-lived.

This part of Martins Wood is managed by coppicing. Coppicing starts by cutting the standard trees off at the base and allowing the remaining bole to sprout for two or three years. The resulting saplings, which may number as many as thirty or forty, are then thinned to allow the remainder to grow into stands of eight or ten centimetres diameter. These are then cut for making into tool handles or fencing stakes. The wood as a whole is carefully managed in areas to ensure a continuous supply of wood over a cycle of twelve to fifteen years. In some woods areas are managed to allow the growth of standard trees to provide larger timber.

Coppicing of woods was more frequent when farming relied more on wood for tools and fencing, but today owners are once again realising the value of a repeating crop of wood.

Another industry which existed side by side with coppicing was the charcoal industry, and camps of charcoal burners were a common sight in the past.

The path eventually arrives at a timber yard. Duck under the barrier gate, keep right across the yard to the track, and follow this to the right. At the fork bear left.

Depending on the time of year - May is a good time - you may be fortunate to hear the rich song of the nightingale, but sightings may be difficult as they usually sing from a perch low in the bushes.

Arriving at a small clearing take the right hand of the two paths that continue in the same direction. (Ignore the paths which go at right angles to the right and left.) The path soon drops down by the side of a few clumps of broom bearing left into a shallow valley. Cross the boggy patch with care to the wooden bridge over the Dodnash brook. (Note the clumps of wild garlic growing profusely on either bank of the stream. A leaf crushed between the fingers will soon reveal the distinctive smell.)

Follow the path up the slope round the edge of the field and then turn left along a wide track bordered by hedge and trees on both sides. This track eventually arrives at the road adjacent to the Grange Caravan and Camp site. Turn left at the road and walk to the hamlet of East End. At the road junction go right to pass the Royal Oak Inn and follow the lane round to the left.

At the next corner leave the lane to take the hedge-lined path which continues in the same direction. On meeting a path which crosses at right angles, turn left and

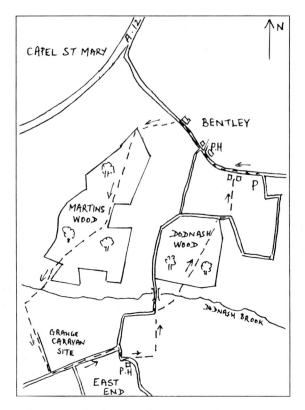

go on until a lane is reached. **Immediately at the bend turn onto the footpath which goes right, and continue across two fields to descend the valley. Cross the bridge and go on up to the stile which leads into Dodnash Wood.**

The water meadow by the bridge is rich in wild flowers. In spring there are many clumps of Cuckoo flower. It gained its name Cuckoo in the sixteenth century either from the fact that the flower bloomed at the time the cuckoo returned and began calling, or from the cuckoo-spit that often covers the flower. This froth, however, is not caused by the cuckoo but by a tiny insect called a frog-hopper. Other names the plant has gained over the years are Milkmaid and Lady's Smock. The flower is pale lilac in colour and is frequent in damp meadows.

The path through the wood is easy to follow and in a short while a road is reached. Here turn right and at the first bend take the footpath on the left. Cross the field and at the hedge go straight forward to pass a house and a small garden nursery to return to the road and the car park.

WALK 19: TWO SUFFOLK VILLAGES
Brandeston to Cretingham

Start: *Brandeston. Grid Ref: 247607. Brandeston lies about 5 miles from Wickham Market.*

O.S.Map: *Landranger 156.*

Distance: *5 miles.*

Time: *2 ½ hours.*

Parking: *Next to the Village Hall, opposite the first thatched cottage on the road to Earl Soham.*

Refreshments: *The Cretingham Bell.*

> *A delightful walk across one of the most beautiful areas in East Suffolk visiting two very attractive villages.*

ON LEAVING THE VILLAGE HALL turn left to go past the terrace of thatched cottages with their eyebrow windows.

> The cottages were part of a 'model' estate adjoining Brandeston Hall, now a preparatory school. One or two of the cottages have the traditional country vegetable garden bordered by flowers and herbaceous plants.

Go past the turning to the Post Office in Mill Lane, once the site of the village mill destroyed by fire in 1893, and in about 20m past the next turning to the right, cross the stile opposite and take the footpath which follows the edge of the small wood on your left.

> In Spring the path here is edged by clumps of cowslips.

Go over a gate and continue forward to enter another wood emerging in a short while to cross a golf course.

Continue on a clearly defined track and at the tee marked by an outsize golf ball bear left towards the clubhouse. When this is reached, keep the club office on the right and go through the small car park to join a track which continues past Grove Farm House to the road.

At the road turn left to pass Manor Farm on the corner with its beautiful copper beech tree (the extension to the house is dated 1855) and at the junction turn left (signposted Brandeston) to enter Cretingham.

The road crosses the River Deben and soon passes St. Peter's Church.

> A welcoming sign invites a visit to a church noteworthy for its box pews and the two-tier pulpit.

Continue in the same direction through the village, past the Bell, and just after the

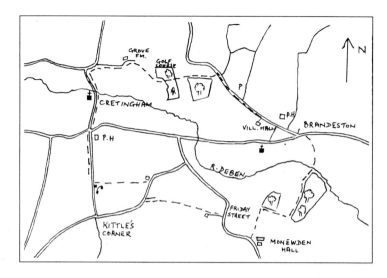

crest of the hill there is a telephone box on the left. **Turn onto the footpath beside the box and go on ahead across two fields to arrive at a lane. Here turn right, and in about 100m turn left to follow a footpath crossing a field. The path soon continues along the right side of a hedge.**

> There are several species of tree and shrub in the hedge including blackthorn, wild rose, spindle, hawthorn, beech and oak, and you may like to test the '30 metre rule'. (See Walk 8)

Carry on over two fields and eventually the path bears right by the side of a small copse towards a farmhouse.

> The house has been in the same family for over three hundred years. Its blocked window on the front aspect is a result of the window tax introduced in Georgian times.

Follow the farm track and turn right when it meets the lane to go past Moat Cottage. At the next bend turn left on to the footpath (do not go past Monewden House unless you want a longer walk returning to Brandeston by road via Kettleburgh). After crossing the stile at the end of the first field turn sharp right along the hedge and, in 100m, cross back over another stile to follow the path by the side of the wood.

In a short while veer to the left of the hedge and continue round the edge of the field. Brandeston Hall (built in 1543) and the church now come into view. The path becomes a track and, after crossing the Deben by a small bridge, continue up a slope bordered on the left by lime trees. At the road junction cross to the second road and turn left to return to the start point.

WALK 20: TO THE GULL AT OTLEY
Otley

Start: *Otley Church. Grid Ref: 204549*
O.S.Map: *Landranger 156*
Distance: 3 ½ *miles*
Time: 1 ½ *hours*
Parking: *Room for one car by the church gate or park further back in the village.*

> *A short walk mainly across farmland beginning and ending at the church. With the possibility of an additional detour to a well-known nearby pottery the walk concludes along the Gull.*

GO THROUGH THE CHURCH GATE and, passing to the right of the church, locate the stile at the back of the churchyard. Cross the stile and in 20m veer right and descend the slope of the field with the hedge on the left. Cross the plank bridge at the bottom and follow the path as it curves round the edge of the wood.

After crossing the bridge turn right, and with the church behind, follow the hedge on the right aiming for the electricity line and the red-roofed cottage ahead. The path meets the lane on the left of the cottage. Here turn left and continue for about half a mile, past a bridge over a stream, until the lane bends sharp right.

At this point a detour may be made to Bernard Rooke's pottery at Swilland. Continue up the lane as far as the B1078. Cross straight over and the pottery is a short way down on the right.

> Rooke's pottery is widely renowned and there is an extensive selection of his work in the studio.

The return detour totals about one mile.

Take the footpath on the left at the bend in the lane (Remember the path will be on the right if returning from the pottery!), pass the edge of a small copse and then turn left towards a farmhouse. Keep on the track between the red barn and the front of the house and then go left of a second barn.

Cross the meadow ahead to a gap in the hedge immediately opposite, then turn left to continue round the edge of the next field to find the path alongside the beginning of The Gull.

> The Gull runs to the left of the path and first appears to be just a stream. Further along the gully deepens into a shallow valley which gradually widens. Both sides of the valley are shrouded in trees and undergrowth with Travellers Joy running riot here and there.
> Travellers Joy, or Old Man's Beard is a member of the Clematis family and

is characteristic in woods on chalk. It could be called our native jungle-creeper and, in winter, trees covered by it take on an almost cob-webbed look from the greyish-white seed heads of the climber. In July it muffles the trees with greenish-white flowers. The name Traveller's Joy was first coined by John Gerard, an Elizabethan gardener, and I wonder whether this name first came to him in the winter or in the summer. Certainly it can be an enthralling sight on a dull winter's day.

Further along still, the valley narrows almost to the width it was at the beginning and the stream becomes hidden by the trees. A Gull, a geological feature to be found in one or two other places in Suffolk, originated from the effects of distortion on the sides of valleys during times of local icefields or permafrost.

The path ends at a metal farm gate and stile. Here turn left and walk back up the road to the church.

Otley Church has many points of interest amongst which is a memorial to a Robert Gosnold whose family seat was at the nearby Otley Hall. Robert was a gentleman usher in the court of Elizabeth I and of James I, and later he became a Privy Councillor to Charles I. Look too for the photograph of an adult baptismal font which was discovered under the floor of the present vestry.

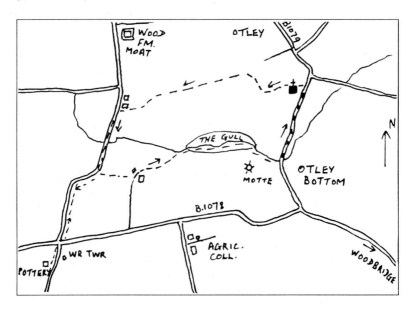

WALK 21: THROUGH FARM AND BY MILL
Saxtead and Earl Soham

Start: *Earl Soham. Grid Ref: 236633*
O.S.Map: *Landranger 156*
Distance: *6 miles*
Time: *3 hours*
Parking: *Space for a car near the church from which the walk starts, or by the village green.*
Refreshments: *The Victoria at Earl Soham or The Volunteer at Saxtead.*

> *This is a relatively easy walk across farmland by way of hedge-lined bridle paths, through woods and fields to the space and peace of Saxtead with its well-preserved post mill. The route back to Earl Soham uses bridle path and country lanes to arrive back near to the church. The walk is well way-marked and there are some splendid views across open country.*

LEAVE THE A1120 by the lane on the right of the church. In 200m, by the nearside of a house and farm buildings, turn right onto a Y.W.M. footpath. At the end of the first hedge turn left and follow the edge of the field round aiming for the electricity pylon and the edge of a copse. The footpath cuts across the field at this point but this may be covered by a crop in summer. 100m short of the copse 'jiggle' left through a gap in the hedge and continue towards the copse.
Keep forward across open farmland where there are extensive views to the right and follow the farm track to the corner. Cross the ditch and bear left along the hedge on a bridleway. In 200m 'jiggle' and continue on the other side of the hedge. Later, ignore the footpath going left and continue along the bridleway.
Then in a short while bear left through the wood.

> Here in the spring the path is edged with an abundance of cuckoo pint with its spear-shaped leaves.

After the wood the path crosses a space and then goes between hedges to meet a lane. Ahead there is a view of Framlingham Church and the battlements of the castle. In 200m, where the lane bends to the left, take the path on the right. Saxtead Mill may be seen to the left. In a short while cross the gap in the hedge on the left and continue forward with the hedge on the right. Ignore the plank bridge which appears on the right and go on over the wider, railed bridge ahead. Bear right and carry on with the hedge and stream on your right. Don't worry about going 'away' from Saxtead. At the next finger-post (No 13) turn left up the rise. Follow the path round to the left towards the mill and a finger-post in the corner of the field. Bear right towards the houses at Saxtead and then keep on this track turning left then right to reach the road.
Turn left to the mill, maybe pausing for refreshment at The Volunteer on the way.

Saxtead Mill

Saxtead Green Mill.

A mill has stood on this spot for over six hundred and fifty years. A Framlingham survey in 1309 reported on the condition of the mill-stones. The present Mill dates from around 1800 but over the years it has seen many alterations. It has been lifted three times to accommodate new machinery, The round house was once only about nine foot to the eaves and the sails swung low enough to hit a pig!

The Mill, which may be visited from Easter through to September (not Sundays), has a three-storey round house and a white-painted buck with a hooded porch. There is a fantail which automatically turned the sails to face the wind. Four patent sails with a span of nearly fifty-five feet originally drove the machinery and mill stones. It was a corn mill until the Great War when it changed to grinding feed stuffs for animals.

Leaving the Mill on the left follow the B1119 towards Saxtead Green (signposted Tannington and Eye). Go past Red House Farm and after the second bend in the road, follow the second footpath on the left towards a white house. Cross the ditch by the house and continue forward to a track. Here turn left and carry on past the lone holly tree to go down a hedge-lined bridleway which eventually arrives at a lane. (ignore a bridleway which goes off to the left.)

In early spring the path here is lined on both sides with primroses. The word Primrose comes from a Latin word meaning 'first rose' - one of the first plants to flower in March. It is particularly common in High Suffolk with its heavier clay soil and many banks and hedgerows are lined with them in this area. Ants are attracted to the food stored in the seeds which are produced, and so help to disperse them. In the Middle Ages the flowers were used in a remedy for gout and rheumatism and even in the making of love potions!

At the road turn left and go on to the next road junction - marked Soham Town Corner on the map. Here bear right and in 20m take the footpath on the right by the side of a bungalow. Continue on this path for some way with the hedge on the left to pass a farm and then a large, grey-brick mansion, Earl Soham Lodge, where the path descends by the side of the adjoining garden. At the foot of the dip bear right with the hedge still on the left. At the end of the field cross the wooden bridge on the left and continue in the same direction. Cross the playing field, going to the right of the school to reach the road and Earl Soham Church.

Of particular interest to visitors to St.Mary's Church will be the double hammer-beam roof and the beautifully carved bench ends which date from the fourteenth century. There is also a Jacobean pulpit complete with tester. The communion rail and Cromwellian alter table (now serving as a side table by the entrance) date from the mid-seventeenth century. In common with many Suffolk churches the exterior is richly decorated with flushwork.

The name Earl Soham originates from a word meaning a marshy area. A local mere was drained as recently as 1970. The village is associated with stories of smugglers on route from Dunwich.

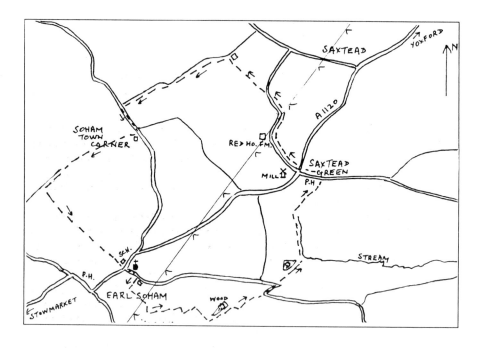

WALK 22: FIELD AND VALLEY
Hintlesham to Burstall

Start: *Hintlesham Church. Grid Ref: 088435*
O.S.Map: *Landranger 155*
Distance: *4½ miles*
Time: *2+ hours*
Refreshments: *The George, Hintlesham.*

A pleasant short walk - the outward half almost entirely across fields, and the return by field and track follows the line of the valley and stream separating the two villages. A walk which proves that Suffolk does have some rolling country-side!

THE FOOTPATH LEAVES THE A1071 at the right-hand side of the churchyard. A narrow path winds its way round the edge of Hintlesham golf course on to a track which leads to a farm. Ignore the footpath leading to the right and go between the farm buildings and to the left of a tall cupressus hedge. Here turn left down the slope and at the bottom keep in the same direction at the side of a bank. Go down by the side of the Alder Carr to a stile.

Cross the stile to a meadow (which can be very wet after prolonged rain) and another stile on the opposite side. Go up the rise and through the right-hand side of the farmyard to the road. Turn left and walk to Burstall Church. Here take the path opposite the church, go through the gate and cross the field to another metal gate. Continue in the same direction, and after the third green gate, the path continues by the hedge and stream on the left of the field. In 50m, after the next

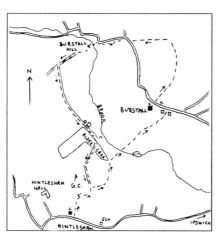

gate, turn left through a double, green gate on to a farm track which leads to the road.

Here turn right and continue along the road for about half a mile to where there is a sharp right hand bend. About 50m further on go over the stile on the left to a footpath and then to a bridge. Cross, and in 100m bear right up the track. At the top of the rise turn left towards Mill Farm at the finger-post.

Keep on this track to eventually pass the farm and at the next junction turn right up the slope. The track then crosses the golf course to return to Hintlesham Church.

WALK 23: ONCE A BUSY PORT
Round and about Orford

Start: *Orford Quay. Grid Ref: 425496*
O.S.Map: *Landranger 169.*
Distance: *3 miles*
Time: *1½ hours*
Parking: *Car Park 50m from the quay.*
Refreshments: *The Jolly Sailor (opposite Car Park). Two more pubs and a well-known fish restaurant in the Square.*

> *A very pleasant walk along the wall of the River Ore returning to the village by track and field. Orford is a most attractive village with the added interest of a fine Norman castle and a church that has a chequered history.*

ON ARRIVING AT THE QUAY turn right on to a path by the shore that leads to the river wall. Continue on the wall for just over a mile.

The wall at this point looks across to Orfordness, a long shingle spit extending over nine miles. In the twelfth century the spit only extended as far as Orford which at that time was an important port. Once, the town had boasted three churches, a friary and two hospitals, but the extension of the spit and the silting up of the port led to its gradual decline as trade transferred to Ipswich.

For a long time during and after the last war, the Ness was a weapons research area and access was restricted. Later it was the site of an early warning system and radio research. The radio masts now transmit the B.B.C. World Service.

At present the future of the Ness as a National Trust conservation area is being planned and perhaps access will become possible once again.

The lighthouse, which is 30m high, dates from the late eighteenth century and is the successor of two previous lights. Its beam extends fifteen miles. The lighthouse became automatic in 1959.

The pagoda-like buildings were used to test trigger mechanisms for atomic weapons. The buildings were designed to collapse to smother an explosion in the event of mishap.

The wall curves right at Chantry Point and overlooks Cuckold's Point, the eastern tip of Havergate Island which is an R.S.P.B. reserve.
Where the river - or The Gull at this point - bends again, bear right on to the track across the fields, and at the lane turn right to return to the village. (A short way along the lane a sandy track goes left and the return to the village can be made this

way. Twenty metres from the barn on the right of the track a footpath cuts straight across the fields to the Castle. Here turn right to reach Quay Street and the Car Park.

Orford was not mentioned in Domesday Book but by the reign of King Stephen the town had been granted a market. The castle was started in 1165 and cost one thousand four hundred pounds, an enormous sum then. The surviving keep is possibly the finest of its kind. Ninety feet high and with walls twenty feet thick, it was the first keep to be built with eighteen external sides - internally it is cylindrical. It was built in this way to counter the under-mining of square corners. The castle is well worth a visit and, on a fine day, there is a superb view from the battlements.

An interesting legend associated with the town and the castle is given in full on the following page..

The tea-room passed on the way to the quay was, at the beginning of this century, a warehouse for storing coal brought to Orford by barge. The village then boasted many shops and at least eight different skilled trades were carried on. Perhaps this was, in part, because the nearby Sudbourne Hall employed many people (including twenty-two gamekeepers!) and the population was much higher than it is now.

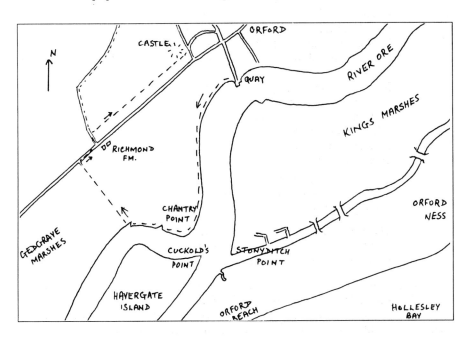

The Wild Man Legend

This was included in the English Chronicle of Ralph of Coggeshall in the thirteenth century.

IN THE TIME OF HENRY II, when Bartholomew de Glanville was keeper of Orford Castle, it happened that fishermen fishing in the sea there caught a wild man in their nets. He was taken to the castle as a marvel. He was entirely naked, and like a human being in all his limbs. But he had hair although it seemed on the surface almost torn away and destroyed. His beard was full and pointed and his chest was extremely hairy and shaggy. The aforesaid knight had him guarded night and day for a long time so that he could not approach the sea. Whatever was brought to him he ate greedily. He ate fish raw as well as cooked, but he wrung out the raw fish in his hands until all the liquid had gone and then he ate them. But he would not utter a word, or rather could not, even though he was hung up by his feet and often severely tortured. When he was taken to a church, he showed not the least sign of reverence or belief, either by kneeling or bowing his head, when he was shown anything holy. He always hurried to his sleeping place at nightfall and slept there until dawn. It happened that they took him once to the harbour and let him loose in the sea, having placed a triple line of very strong nets across the harbour. He soon made for the depths of the sea, passing all the nets, and repeatedly came up from deep water, gazing at those who were watching him from the shore for a very long time, often diving down and re-appearing after a moment, as though he were mocking those who watched him because he had escaped from their nets.

He played like this in the sea for a long while and everyone had given up hope that he would return, but he came back of his own accord to them, swimming through the waves, and remained with them for another two months. But after this he was less carefully guarded, and he now disliked his way of life. So he secretly slipped down to the sea and never appeared again.

Whether this was a mortal man or some kind of fish pretending to be a human being or some evil spirit lurking in the body of a drowned man it is not easy to see, particularly because so many people tell such marvellous tales about this kind of event

WALK 24: A NINETEENTH CENTURY MURDER
In and around Polstead

Start: *Polstead. Grid Ref: 990382*
O.S.Map: *Landranger 155*
Distance: *3 miles*
Time: *1 ½ hours*
Parking: *By the pond. If space is full, an alternative is by the stile opposite the end of Mill Street (on the route of the walk) half a mile towards Stoke-by-Nayland.*
Refreshments: *The Cock Inn.*

> *This walk first follows the route associated with the notorious Red Barn murder which took place in 1827 and then continues to the south east of the village, through woods and across fields, returning along the valley of the River Box. It traverses some of the most beautiful countryside in Suffolk*

START BY CROSSING the bridge on the right of Polstead pond. If parking by Mill Street, walk into the village and turn right up the hill at the side of the pond.

Polstead, from a word meaning 'a place of pools' takes its name from the two ponds. The large amount of Roman material used in the building of the church points to the village extending back at least to this period.

A short way up the hill on the right is Street Farm or Corder's House, a tall gabled house which, in the nineteenth century, was owned by a farmer, John Corder. He had four sons, the third of whom was William, born in 1803. The events which occurred in the years 1826 and 1827 are now necessarily clouded by time, but it would seem that William Corder enjoyed the high life and was not the best of sons. He formed a relationship with a local girl, Maria Marten, who had already borne two illegitimate children, and this resulted in the birth of another child.

Continue up the hill as far as The Green which is overlooked by The Cock Inn. On the right, just before the green look for a footpath which is almost hidden by a hedge. Go down this path and keep on over the estate road aiming for Stoke by Nayland Church seen on the skyline. Cross the field and go down the narrow path as far as the road. Here turn left and, in 30m at Bell's Corner, turn left again along the lane to Shelly. Pass three cottages, the first of which was once The Eight Bells Inn, and a little further on, where the lane bends slightly, is a thatched cottage with two dormer windows.

This is the cottage where Maria lived with her parents and three sisters. Born in 1801, Maria was sent, at a very early age, to Layham to work as a servant - obviously to supplement the wage brought in by her father who

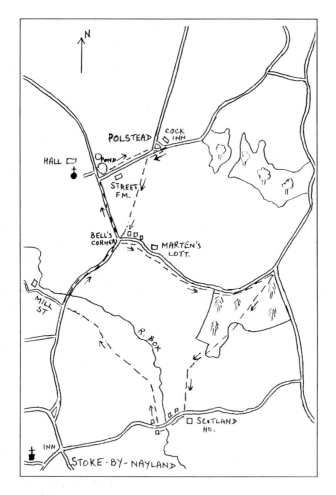

was employed as a molecatcher. Later she had to return home to care for her younger sisters when her mother died.

The child she bore to William died after a few weeks but it is thought that Maria and her parents (her father had re-married) insisted that William marry Maria. It was at this cottage that he came ostensibly to take Maria to Ipswich to get married. It is said that Maria had to hide her identity from the villagers before they left the cottage by dressing in man's clothing. They went on up the hill to the heath where William said he had a horse and gig ready.

Continue up the hill past the entrance to Cherry Tree Farm to where the lane levels out and there are views over the countryside to the left.

In this neighbourhood was the site of the Red Barn where Maria was to change and begin the journey to Ipswich. Here she was murdered and her body buried under the floor of the barn.

William later deceived the parents that Maria was alive and well in Ipswich. Her stepmother became more and more anxious and the story goes that she dreamed that Maria was dead and had been buried in the Red Barn. This was investigated and found to be true and as a result William, who had since married another woman, was tried for the murder and convicted. He was hanged at Bury St.Edmunds in August 1828 before a large crowd.

The Red Barn has long since disappeared, vandalised initially by souvenir hunters at the time as was the tombstone of Maria Marten who was buried in Polstead churchyard in April 1828. A wooden plaque there is her only memorial. The Red Barn was finally destroyed by fire in 1842.

Carry on along the lane to a junction with the road to Stoke. Look for a footpath sign at the edge of the wood on the right and follow the path diagonally through the wood. Where it meets another path continue straight over to cross an open

Polstead from the village pond

space by farm buildings. **Re-enter the wood to drop down a slope to a stile. Cross the stile, bear left for 20m, and then right down the side of the hill towards the River Box. Cross a bridge and stile and go left to meet the lane at Scotland House. Here turn right and in a short while, just past a wall post-box, take the footpath on the right. Go round the edge of the field, 'jiggle' to the other side of the hedge, and continue ahead across fields to reach the road by Mill Street. (The first house along this street is the converted mill with its granary loft.) Turn right to return to the village.**

Opposite Polstead pond is a path leading to St.Mary's Church which I consider to be one of the most beautiful in Suffolk because of its position overlooking the vale, its unique interior and its quiet serenity. The interior is notable for its Norman arches of stepped bricks. There is much else to make a visit to this cared-for church well worthwhile.

Field and Woodland Birds

An alphabetical check list of the commoner birds to be seen in the area including some birds of prey. Space is provided at the end to include other sightings.

Species	Date spotted	Species	Date spotted
Blackbird		Owl, Little	
Blackcap		Robin	
Carrion Crow		Rook	
Chaffinch		Sand Martin	
Chiffchaff		Skylark	
Coot		Siskin	
Cuckoo		Sparrowhawk	
Dove, Collared		Starling	
Dove, Turtle		Stonechat	
Fieldfare		Swallow	
Goldfinch		Swift	
Harrier, Hen		Tit, Blue	
Harrier, Marsh		Tit, Great	
Hedge Sparrow		Tit, Longtailed	
House Sparrow		Thrush, Mistle	
House Martin		Thrush, Song	
Jay		Wagtail, Pied	
Kestrel		Wagtail, Yellow	
Kingfisher		Warbler, Reed	
Lapwing		Warbler, Sedge	
Linnet		Warbler, Willow	
Magpie		Woodpigeon	
Meadow Pipit		Wren	
Moorhen		Yellowhammer	

River and Estuary Birds

Waders & Gulls		Wildfowl	
Species	Date spotted	Species	Date spotted
Avocet		Gadwall	
Curlew		Goose, Canada	
Dunlin		Goose, Greylag	
Godwit		Mallard	
Gull, Black-headed		Mute Swan	
Gull, Herring		Pochard	
Gull, Lesser Blackback		Shelduck	
Gull, Greater		Shoveler	
Grey Plover		Teal	
Heron		Tufted Duck	
Knot		Widgeon	
Oystercatcher			
Redshank			
Ringed Plover			
Ruff			
Sandpiper, Common			
Tern, Common			
Tern, Little			

Butterflies

Below is a list of the commoner varieties of butterflies to be found in Suffolk with brief notes of the usual habitat and the period when they are on the wing.

Species	Habitat	On wing	Common Area
Small Skipper	Field and woodland edges, heathland, cliffs, roadside verges, derelict areas. Areas with wild grasses.	June and July	Widespread esp. Sandlings
Essex Skipper	Areas of wild grass esp. cocksfoot. Verges & embankments.	July	High Suffolk. Sandlings
Large Skipper	Areas of wild grass esp. cocksfoot but prefers damp areas in woods, riverside and meadow. Perches on leaves of bramble and bracken.	Mid June+	Widespread
Clouded Yellow	Areas of clover, trefoil and vetches.	June to Aug.	Uncommon but has good years.
Brimstone	Woodland edges and verges where there are flowers esp. Knapweed.	April onwards but young adults July-Sept.	Mainly West Suffolk, possible in South
Large White	Particularly amongst cabbage crops and nasturtiums.	Late April-Sept. 2 broods.	Widespread
Small White	As above	Late April-Oct 2 to 3 broods.	Widespread
Green-Veined White	Damp places but may be seen anywhere. Often feeds on Hedge Mustard, Rape and other crucifers.	May to Sept.	Widespread
Orange Tip	Hedgerows. Flower heads particularly Jack-by-the-Hedge, Black Mustard, Lady's Smock.	May to early July	Widespread. esp. South & East Suffolk.
Small Copper	Heather, Ragwort and Yarrow, bare earth and conifer forest. Darting flight.	Late April to October. 3 broods	East Suffolk esp. Sandlings
Common Blue	Derelict land and heaths. Cliffs and shingle. Gravel pits. Embankments.	Late May to Sept. 2 broods.	Widespread esp. South & Sandlings
Holly Blue	Hedgerows, woodland glades and edges. A blue seen before Mid-May will be a Holly Blue.	Late April to Sept. 2 broods.	Common in South Suffolk.

Red Admiral	Woods, parkland and gardens. Lays eggs on stinging nettles. Attracted by buddleia, Michaelmas Daisies and Ivy flowers.	Late May to September	Common in South and East. Less in High Suffolk.
Painted Lady	Prefers open ground, Thistles, Stinging nettles & Burdock. Black-tipped wings with white spots but orangey pink rather than red.	June to Oct.	Mainly along the coast.
Small Tortoiseshell	As for Red Admiral	Overwinters. 2 broods.	Very common.
Peacock	Stinging nettles, Knapweed, Field Scabious & Buddleia. Four peacock eyes.	April-June. Late July to Oct. 2 broods.	Very common
Comma	Mainly woodlands but also gardens attracted by Buddleia and Daisies. Nettles.	April to Sept. 2 broods.	Anywhere, but more often South and East.
Speckled Wood	Woodland edges, tracks and glades where there is light and shade. Grasses and Ragwort.	April to Oct.	Mainly in North-West Suffolk.
Wall	Poor soils as for Common Blue. Grasses, Shingle.	May to Sept.	South & Sandlings. Breckland.
Grayling	Grassland on poor soils with bare areas. Sheltered areas in conifer woods. Thistles and heathers. When disturbed, flies off erratically to soon settle again.	July to Sept.	Sandlings.
Gatekeeper or Hedge Brown	Hedgerows, field and woodland edges and verges. Grasses.	July & Aug.	Very common.
Meadow Brown	Habitat as above. Knapweed, brambles, grasses. Slow flapping flight.	June to Sept.	Very common
Small Heath	Poorer soils of heaths, coastal areas, verges and banks, quarries, conifer woods, shingle.	May to Sept.	Sandlings.
Ringlet	Damp sheltered areas and tall grass along hedges and forest tracks. Grasses.	July to Aug.	Widespread.

List of Trees and Shrubs for hedge dating

Alder

Apple

Ash

Beech

Blackthorn

Briar

Broom

Buckthorn

Cherry

Cherry-plum

Dogwood

Elder

Elm: Wych, English, etc.

Furze

Guelder-rose

Hawthorn: hedgerow, woodland

Hazel

Holly

Hornbeam

Lime: ordinary, pry

Maple

Oak: pedunculate, sessile

Pine

Plum

Poplar: Aspen, Black, White

Privet (wild)

Rowan

Sallow

Service

Spindle

Sycamore

Wayfaring tree

Whitebeam

Willow: crack, white

Yew

Coppicing and bluebells in Martins Wood, Bentley

Suffolk Wildlife Trust Reserves

Reserve	Description	Grid Ref.	Access
Blackenham, Chalk Pits	Grassland and chalk-loving species.	TM109490	Open Days only
Blakes Meadow, Dallinghoo	Small meadow, old hedges, pond.	TM272552	All Times
Blaxhall Heath	Sandlings	TM380565	All Times
Bonny Wood, Barking Tye	Ancient Wood, flowers	TM076520	All Times
Bromeswell Green	Woodland and reedbed	TM296504	All Times
Bucklesham Road Heath	Sandlings heathlands	TM199429	All Times
Combs Wood	Ancient coppiced wood, wild flowers and birds	TM054568	All Times
Darsham Marshes	Dykes, pond, wildflowers	TM420691	All Times
Fox Fritillary Meadow	Fritillaries	TM190607	All Times sign book at farm.
Framlingham Mere	Lake, marsh next to Framlingham College.	TM284638	All Times
Groton Wood, Nr. Sudbury	Ancient woodland. Limes	TL976428	All Times
Hascot Pit	Geology Site of Pleistocene Period.	TM062539	All Times
Hollesley Heath	Heath, woodland, Nightjars.	TM347466	By permission of the warden
Landguard Point, Felixstowe	Migratory birds. Shingle spit. Coastal plants.	TM284320	All Times
Levington Lagoon	Wildfowl, Waders	TM239385	All Times
Nacton Meadows	Wet meadows, flowers, insects (path from Levington to Amberfield School)	TM232400	All Times
Newbourne Springs	Eroded valley. Spring-fed stream. Woodland birds.	TM271433	All Times

Norman Gwatkins, Nr.Southwold	Marsh, reedbeds. Hides.	TM463767	All Times
Potash Lane Hedge	Historic hedge. 1000 years old	TL993404-2	All Times
Reydon Wood	Ancient coppice, bluebells, yellow archangel.	TM476790	All Times
Spring Wood, SW Ipswich	Small ancient woodland	TM144414	All Times

Butley River

Notable R.S.P.B. Reserves

Reserve	Description	Grid Ref.	Access
Butley River	Small reserve bordering river	TM392482	All times.
Minsmere	Woodland, Meres, Marsh. Harriers.	TM472672	Permit rqd. Closed Tue.
Wolves Wood, Nr. Hadleigh	Old woodland, part managed. Nightingales.	TM054436	All times
Havergate Island, Orford	Wildfowl, waders, owls.	TM415475	(advance bookings)
North Warren	Birchwood, heather.	TM455587	All times

How to read a Grid Reference

TO HELP PINPOINT a place on the ground all Ordnance Survey maps are divided into small squares by vertical and horizontal lines or Grid lines. These lines are numbered and in a six figured reference the first three figures refer to the number of the vertical lines or Eastings and the last three to the horizontal lines or Northings.

Take the point on the sample map of Benacre Church.

First quote the Eastings.
Find the first vertical line to the left of the church and read the large figures at the end of the line at the top or bottom of the map, in this case - 51
Estimate in tenths of a square from the grid line to the church, i.e. 2

Then quote the Northings.
Find the first horizontal line below the church and read the figures at the end of the line at the right or left margin of the map, in this case - 84
Estimate in tenths of a square from the grid line to the church, i.e. 4

The sample reference is therefore 512 844

Following the same method give grid references for the Hall in Benacre Park and for Blackmoor Farm, Nr. Wrentham.

Benacre Hall   502 837   Blackmoor Farm   488 834

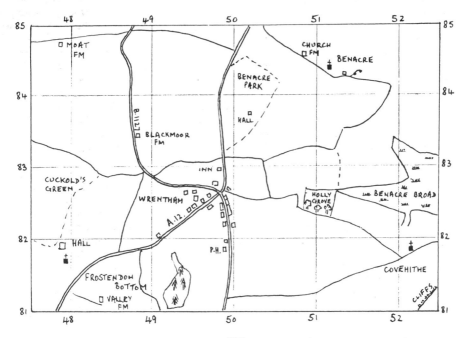

About the Author

JOHN PARDY moved to Suffolk 25 years ago with his wife Vivien and daughter Jess. Their first home was a coastguard cottage on the beach at Shingle Street. The Suffolk coast, its wildlife and history inspired an interest in walking and the discovery of places only accessible on foot. Following early retirement from his job as Headteacher of a Primary School, John now has time to record his walks and develop his other interests in music, birdwatching and gardening. Now living in a village on the Felixstowe peninsula, he is considered an authority on walking in Suffolk and shares his walks with friends in the area and also his dog, Ben.

Bibliography

Ager, D.V.	Introducing Geology	Faber. 1961
Arnott, W.G.	Suffolk Estuary.	N.Adlard. 1950
Arnott, W.G.	Orwell Estuary	Boydell Press. 1954
Arnott, W.G.	Alde Estuary	N.Adlard. 1952
Blythe, R.	Akenfield	Allen Lane. 1969
Dymond, D	(Ed) An Historical Atlas of Suffolk	S.C.C. 1988
Evans, A.	Sutton Hoo Ship Burial	British Museum. 1986
Evans, G.E.	Ask the Fellows Who Cut the Hay	Faber. 1956
Fletcher, R.	The East Anglians	P.Stephens. 1980
Jobson, A.	Suffolk Villages	R.Hale. 1971
Haining, P.	Maria Marten - The Murder in the Red Barn	Richard Castell. 1992
Hollom, P.A.D.	The Popular Handbook of British Birds	Witherby. 1968
Hoskins, W.G.	The Making of the English Landscape	Hodder & Stoughton. 1988
Mendel, H. etc.	The Butterflies of Suffolk	Suffolk Naturalists. 1986
Pevsner, N.	The Buildings of England - Suffolk	Penguin. 1961
Rackham, O.	The History of the Landscape	J.M.Dent. 1986
Readers Dig.	Field Guide to the Wild Flowers of Britain	Readers Digest Ass. 1981
Reynolds, M.J.	(Ed.) About Suffolk	Boydell. 1978
Scarfe, N.	The Suffolk Landscape	Hodder & Stoughton. 1972
S.F.W.I.	The Suffolk Village Book	Countryside Books. 1991
Simper, R.	The Suffolk Sandlings	East Anglian Daily Times. 1986
Simper, R.	The Deben River	Creekside Publishing. 1992
Simpson, F.W.	Flora of Suffolk	Suffolk Naturalists. 1982
S.W.T.	The Suffolk Estuaries	S.W.T. 1988
Thomas, J.A.	Butterflies of the British Isles	Hamlyn. 1986
Wilson, D.	A Short History of Suffolk	Batsford. 1977

Love lives beyond.

'Tis seen in flowers,
And in the morning's pearly dew;
In the earth's green hours,
And in the heaven's eternal blue.

John Clare